HAPPY CLOUD MEDIA

EXPLOITATION NATION

CW00828061

Exploitation Nation is published by Happy Cloud Media, LLC
Vol. 1, No. 2 © 2017

Amy Lynn Best, Publisher
Mike Watt, Editor
Carolyn Haushalter, Asst. Editor

Contributors:
Bill Adcock
Dr. Rhonda Baughman
Mike Haushalter
Bill Hahner
Douglas Waltz
William Wright

Cover art designed by
Phillip Rogers

Logo created by
Ryan Hose

Special Thanks to:
Pete Chiarella
Steven Bejma
Janet Rogers
Mike Raso
Paige K. Davis

An Unspeakable Horror of a Podcast
http://www.mortismedia.com/

https://www.facebook.com/Secretscrolldigest

http://divineexploitation.blogspot.com/

DOWN THE RABBIT HOLE

Exploitation Nation prides itself on being a democratic publication. So when I opened up suggestions for the theme of issue two, I was a little surprised that the "Bigfoot/Cryptozoology" subgenre received so many votes. I keep forgetting that my taste isn't necessarily the final word when it comes to obscure cinema. See, I'm not a Bigfoot fan, nor a believer. But then again, I don't have to be. Plenty of people are, and that's okay.

George A. Romero, the patron saint of horror filmmakers, passed away on Sunday, July 16, 2017. Because I am a Pittsburgh filmmaker and knew Mr. Romero slightly, within hours of the announcement of his passing, I received several phone calls from local media asking me to write something in tribute. I assembled three separate pieces into what follows below. It's the best way I know to good-bye to George.

You may notice a bit of honesty that may become a permanent feature here at Exploitation Nation, namely the "Page Count Padding Department". It's true. This issue, as with the last, came up a bit short in the page count department. Fortunately, inspiration struck while flipping through Netflix and seeing *Sorority Row* up in the queue. *Sorority Row* was one of the first "big" set visits I'd ever done and it was a learning experience for a lot of reasons, first and foremost that it came at the end of my brief tenure at Fangoria. Long the goal of my journalism career, I landed in "Be careful what you wish for" territory as I managed to land a few gigs there just as their monetary problems had really begun to kick in. The possibility of my not being paid for this all-day gig, one which I'd have to take off from my day job to cover, was a very real one. Fortunately, Tony Timpone came through for me, though it would be my last paid piece at Fango.

Ironically, just as I decided to revisit the piece, I discovered that all of my files between 2009 and 2010 have vanished from all my archives. That was a significant "donwtime" period in my journalism career, so nothing major was lost, but confounding this situation was being unable to find the magazine containing the issue (#287, just for reference). I suddenly couldn't remember if I'd ever even had one. It was tough to even get comp copies out of Fango at the time, my friendship with Michael Gingold of no standing or consequence. So that was frustrating.

What you get with "Page Count Padding" this issue is an annotated version of the original article that appeared in #287. I wish I could find my original transcriptions--Leah Pipes and Briana Evigan in particular gave highly entertaining interviews and it would have been nice to present some of the content that had remained unpublished. Maybe I'll luck out or maybe I'll go mad and revisit the audio files that still remain on my little digital recorder.

But I wouldn't hold my breath on that one.

--Mike Watt, September, 2017.

REMEMBERING GEORGE A. ROMERO
By Mike Watt

He was known affectionately and colloquially as "The Godfather of the Zombie Movie," thanks to a little black-and-white shocker he'd co-written, co-produced and directed in 1969, *Night of the Living Dead*. Created in the hopes of making a modest return in order to fund more high-minded art films, George Romero, John A. Russo, Russell Streiner and seven other members of the "Latent Image" team created something that will outlive us all. A small group of panicked humans, trapped inside a dilapidated Pennsylvania farmhouse surrounded by a ravenous horde of reanimated corpses, each other's instincts conflicting—sometimes violently—as they struggle to survive the night. It was intentionally evocative of Richard Matheson's classic tale, *I Am Legend*, but it became so much more.

At first, the film was reviled by critics comparing it to base porno-graphy, thanks to the unflinching sequences of cannibalism and violence. Because of its black-and-white presentation, the movie had a documentary feel: "you are here, this is now." Audiences weren't quite ready for its arrival. Not at first. But after a few weeks of playing in local theaters and drive-ins, *Night of the Living Dead* didn't go away.

Part of the film's legacy is borne on the shoulders of its lead, Duane Jones, an African American actor chosen to play the film's hero, Ben, based on the strength of his audition and not because of the color of his skin. Yet, it proved to be a landmark creative decision during the height of the Civil Rights clashes occurring daily throughout the United States. Ben's race is never addressed in the film, no slurs are used against him during the heated arguments. This in

Above: George A. Romero. Photographer unknown. All Rights Reserved

itself was groundbreaking: the black man was on equal footing with his white compatriots, because the world was ending around them. Race was secondary to survival.

The hungry ghouls devouring the living were retroactively compared to the creeping threat of Communism. Later, a conscious choice would be made to use the ghouls as parables for rampant consumerism (in the color follow-up *Dawn of the Dead*); in *Day of the Dead*, they were now the dominant race on the planet, with healthy living humans driven underground, hiding in bunkers and waiting for the inevitable. *Day* was filmed in 1985 and then, for a while, movie theaters were relatively zombie-free.

His influence, however, can hardly be understated. *Night of the Living Dead*, for all of its detractors, legitimized horror for adult audiences. Long relegated to the stature of tax dodges and weekend shoots for the burgeoning teenage drive-in market, horror was despised prior to 1969, particularly by critics who saw no value. After *Night of the Living Dead*, attitudes changed. Look no further than the lasting global success of *The Exorcist*. Romero's influence is all over that film in terms of stylistic choices on the part of director William Friedkin—so much of the first act shot documentary style—and the tonal choice of "this is happening, this is real, this could happen to you." Look at Stephen Spielberg's *Jaws*, the juggernaut that invented the Summer Blockbuster. So much of the movie has the shark unseen, a constant lurking menace, while the protagonists struggle to communicate and work with each other. Filmmakers were discovering new ways to both terrify the audience and make them question the world around them. Who has our best interests in mind? Who are we in times of crisis? Are any of us really as strong as we pretend to be? All of these used to be the domain of the serious drama. Now they're coated in misdirection—the blood and horror the primary lure, the critique of civilization a bitter pill coated in candy trappings.

There will never be another filmmaker like George A. Romero, nor should there be, nor should we *want* there to be. His movies were the singular product of an excited mind, someone who saw an established genre and, to use an overextended phrase, *reinvented it* for his own devices. Without Romero, there would be no *Resident Evil*, there would be no *Walking Dead*. Without the love of those who grew up on *Night, Dawn*, and *Day*, zombies wouldn't be the cultural phenomenon they are today.

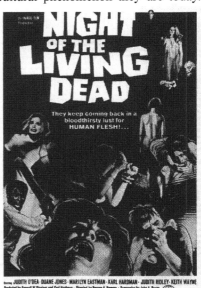

and *Survival*. The latter three came and of the *Dead*. Creepshow's *Tom Savini*, who'd created all the

late in his career, but growing up we horror fans devoured the first three and hoarded the scarce memorabilia, the *Fangoria* and *Cinefantastique* movie mags splashing the gory bits across the covers.

Between *Day* and his "comeback", *Land*, George created a number of fun and oftentimes terrifying films. He was one of the very first filmmakers to study the vampire story from outside the mythological trappings in *Martin*, with John Amplas giving a marvelous turn to a troubled young man who suffers from a blood-drinking addiction. George's elegiac *Knightriders*, about a troupe of pseudo-Renaissance actors on motorcycles traveling to fairgrounds and staging jousting matches on motorcycles, is probably his most personal work, featuring standout performances by Ed Harris and George's protégé,

imaginatively-disgusting gore effects for *Dawn, Martin*, and *Day*.

Perhaps Romero's finest work came as a collaboration with the world's most successful horror author, Stephen King. Though Romero directed a straight adaptation of King's difficult *The Dark Half*, it was their friendship and mutual love of EC Comics that propelled *Creepshow* to the classic status it holds today. Lurid, colorful, vivid, shocking *and* scary and hilarious at times, *Creepshow* is all things for all horror fans, perfectly evoking the spirit and flavor of the classic anthology films like *Tales from the Crypt* and *Vault of Horror*, the effects and gruesomeness off the charts. The enthusiasm pours from the screen as each *Creepshow* unfolds. This particular bottled lightning was never recaptured, not in the two sequels that followed and not in the countless others that came after.

Following the odd and inaccessible *Bruiser* in 2000, Romero's output became sporadic. That film's box office failure sent the typical signal to Hollywood that Romero's brand of unique disquiet was no longer in fashion. As usual, the ill-considered dictum became law and the director found financing increasingly difficult to achieve. For years, he shopped and developed a ghost story entitled *Black Mariah*, as well as an expensive, apocalyptic new chapter in his *Dead* series, this time named after the story's central character, a rolling battle tank nicknamed "Dead Reckoning," and the ragtag team of mercenaries cleaning up pockets of zombie incursion. For a long time, it looked as if his bizarre horror rock-opera, *The Diamond Dead*, would come to life and relaunch a *Rocky Horror*-esque movement, but funding collapsed and the project died with it. Then in 2004, with an expensive remake of his seminal *Dawn of the Dead* in the pipeline with the big studios, he finally got the greenlight for *Dead Reckoning*, now retitled *Land of the Dead*.

For many, *Land* was either a return to form or a diluted and slick late entry into the series. Made with a fraction of the budget granted Zack Snyder and his dizzying *Dawn* remake (his decision to make running zombies the center of a raging debate to this day), *Land of the Dead* was a "greatest hits" of the previous films, with the added additions of bigger stars—*The Mentalist*'s Simon Baker, counterculture hero Dennis Hopper, and Asia Argento, daughter of Romero's Italian counterpart Dario (who reedited *Dawn of the Dead* as *Zombie* for Italian audiences in 1979). It wasn't a great success financially, but it heralded Romero's return to the cinema.

For Pittsburgh, *Land* was Romero's coming home. Though filmed in Canada, Pittsburghers retained their proprietary attitude that Romero was one of them, a hometown boy made good. Because of George, Pittsburgh is the "Zombie Capital of the World," attracting visitors from all over the globe eager to visit The Monroeville Mall, made famous in his *Dawn*, or the Evans City Cemetery figuring so prominently in *Night*. That these places no longer even resemble the locations in the film causes no concern. And to celebrate Pittsburgh's Patron Saint of the Undead, his son, Cameron, a filmmaker himself, organized the biggest film premiere the city has ever seen. For the *Land of the Dead* premiere, one hot day in June saw the arrival of all those who held George in

the highest esteem. Not just "regular" Pittsburghers, but huge talents in their own right: Quentin Tarantino, Robert Rodriguez, Simon Pegg, Edgar Wright (the pair behind the Romero love-letter, *Shawn of the Dead*), director and effects artist Robert Kurtzman and future *Walking Dead* director and Romero protégé Greg Nicotero—all walked down the Benedum's red carpet, greeted by ushers decked out in zombie make-up.

And when Romero was introduced by his son, 3,000 people stood to applaud, to thank the man with clapping hands for all he'd done. For the world, for Pittsburgh, for horror in general. After the film, a huge after-party was held and even basketball great Michael Jordan made an appearance to show appreciation.

We all thought, after *Land*, that we'd see some of the non-zombie films he'd been working towards for so many years. But *Land* didn't break the box-office bank and he was left again to his own devices. No ghost stories, no musicals. We'd get two more "legitimate" Romero zombie films—the mockumentary *Diary of the Dead* and the pseudo-Western, *Survival of the Dead*. Hollywood leeched what it could of his legacy and gave us slick remakes of *The Crazies,* disastrous updates of *Day of the Dead*, and multiple disposable versions of *Night.* Like so many men of vision before him—George Pal springs instantly to mind—the studios wanted nothing more than "Romero-like", but didn't have a use for the man himself.

I could go on about how Hollywood co-opted his flesh-eating ghouls time and again without paying tribute. Indeed, at the very time *The Walking Dead* became a money-making phenomenon for AMC and comic creator Robert Kirkman, Romero struggled to find financing for zombie films of his own. When the expensive remake of his seminal *Dawn of the Dead* splashed across theater screens across the country, his own modestly-budged *Land of the Dead* could find

Above: Ken Foree and Tom Savini in Romero's Knightriders.
Photo Copyright Laurel Productions. All Rights Reserved.

only limited distribution. The irony was only lost on the suits in charge. The man who created the demand for the remake couldn't find cash for his own unique ideas. There was more value to be found in the rehash, not the continuation.

But it was *Land* that showed me who the man was through the eyes of those who loved him. My own personal encounters with the gentleman were largely professional. I'd see him at conventions, having known his manager for many years, having shared mutual friends for most of my own career. My first personal introduction came via his son, Cameron, with whom my wife and I had developed a professional relationship that had burgeoned into a friendship. At a Pittsburgh horror convention, where George and Cameron were promoting a unique proposed horror-musical titled *The Diamond Dead*, Cam embraced us warmly and said, "This is my Dad." George treated us like we were longtime friends of his own. But we were quickly interrupted by the demands of his time and from the long line of other people desperate to meet their hero.

In 2005, Amy, my wife, and I got to participate in the biggest love letter any son has ever given his father. Cameron and his business partners threw a gala for the premiere of George's latest, his return to the zombie genre he'd helped create and certainly developed. It was well-known that *Land* hadn't been his first choice for a career return—he'd tried unsuccessfully for years to develop a ghost story titled *Black Mariah*, and *Land* was from a script titled *Dead Reckoning*, paired down from its originally apocalyptic imagining. But it was still a huge deal for fans, who by now numbered thousands of other filmmakers including the British inheritors, Edgar Wright and Simon Pegg (both of whom appear in the final film as very recognizable zombies).

Cameron wanted Pittsburgh to know how great a debt the horror film industry owed to his father. Over the course of a very few weeks, Cam and his partners contacted every major industry player they could think of. For the premiere at the opulant Benedum Center for the Performing Arts in Pittsburgh, ushers were made up as rotting ghouls and a red carpet was rolled out for the visiting dignitaries, including Quentin Tarantino, Robert Rodriguez, Pegg, Wright, Savini and his own made-good prodigy Greg Nicotero (now one of the principal show-runners on *The Walking Dead*), effects artist and director Robert Kurtzman, and, later, basketball great Michael Jordan. The auditorium was filled front to back to balcony with giddy fans. When George was introduced, he received a standing ovation.

And it was humbling. Nearly three thousand people from all walks of life—fans, pros, admirers—standing and applauding for a humble man in comically-large eye glasses, a gentle, smiling grandfatherly type who'd spent most of his life trying to figure out new and spectacular ways for people to die. A man who knew that horror without content was just shock. His characters suffered great losses, but always something else was going on. *Martin* was more about untreated schizophrenia and xenophobia than it was vampirism; *Knightriders* was personal standards of righteousness and community at great risk to self and safety; his classic ghoul trilogy is about the degradation of a society ill-equipped for cataclysmic change—the zombies could have been a metaphor for damned near anything and everything and critics have been making arguments for and against since 1969. This isn't even to mention his frequent collaboration with horror author and phenomenon Stephen King, particularly their own love-letter to EC Comics, the garish four-colored anthology film, *Creepshow*, which many hold as their favorite Romero film. There are also *The Dark Half* (another King adaptation), the creepy *Monkey Shines* (about a quadriplegic held at the mercy of his psychotic helper monkey—it's scarier than it sounds), and his most bizarre and least accessible *Bruiser*, about the ego-crushing world of magazine publishing (possibly, the film is fairly esoteric and was not well-received).

In the end, Hollywood had determined that a remake of *The Crazies* would be a better financial move than hiring the original director to do something unique. Romero would struggle hard even to get money for the "found footage" zombie film, *Diary of the Dead* (which felt more like the master aping those who'd come after him); his final film, *Survival of the Dead*, plays more like a western than anything else, where the zombies are the victims this time, caught in a feud between two families. More than one critic has pointed out that it seemed Romero was far more interested in the familial interplay—the "Western" elements—than he was in doing yet another chapter of the shuffling, shambling corpses now developing a sentience of their own. His creations were still evolving, even if the genre itself was starting to stagnate. Without the metaphor, zombies are just targets or a biting mass of threat. Romero gave them back their souls.

None of that mattered in 2005. Only the applauding throng, there because a son loved his father more

Romero with friends at Cine Vegas, June 18, 2005, at the Palms Hotel and Casino in Las Vegas. Photographer Unknown. All Rights Reserved.

10

than he could express through words. They'd had a complicated relationship, but even that didn't matter during that moment, with George on stage, blushing from the applause.

As filmmakers, we couldn't help but feel George's influence. In our first film, we payed direct and unsubtle homage to *Night of the Living Dead*, shooting our opening sequence in black and white to best emulate one of the most famous openings in history: siblings Johnny and Barbara visiting the graves of their mother, only to be beset by a gaunt walking corpse, the late Bill Hinzman. But as human beings, we saw George A. Romero the fellow human being, the elder statesman whose art had affected the uncountable. Whatever Hollywood had taken from him and never gave back, nothing was missing from him that night. He never snubbed a fan, never accepted a compliment with arrogance. People who knew him better will be paying tribute over these next few difficult days of shock and grief; I only knew him as an artist and a man whose son idolized him. And I feel grateful enough for that.

"The Father of the Modern Zombie Film" passed away on Sunday. Of course, he was so much more than that, but legacies are tricky things. He'll always be celebrated for his imagination and his many groundbreaking films, but he was also a father, a husband, a warm and welcoming friend, a patient teacher, a kind soul.

Photo Copyright Laurel Entertainment. All Rights Reserved.

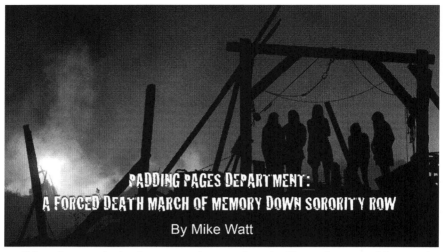

PADDING PAGES DEPARTMENT:
A FORCED DEATH MARCH OF MEMORY DOWN SORORITY ROW
By Mike Watt

It's the typical horror-movie situation: A young woman, dressed in only what she sleeps in, makes her way cautiously, nervously, through the dark house. Past the spiral staircase leading upstairs, past the entryway into the pitch-black kitchen, tentatively she calls the names of her friends. A figure, dressed in a black robe and hood, steps out of the shadows behind her. She freezes as he holds up a weapon—a Molotov cocktail—and hurls it at her head as she runs screaming from the room. The curtains ignite, the figure pursues...

The assistant director yells "Cut," director Stewart Hendler, seated behind his monitor, smiles wide and a wardrobe assistant throws a robe around the shoulders of the scantily clad actress, Caroline D'Amore. Firemen with CO_2 canisters have already doused the flames, and the rest of the crew scurry around, ready to reset. The atmosphere is all business, but minus the tension you'd normally find on a set like this. Most of the people working are smiling—even the notoriously taciturn Pittsburgh

grips. As Fango is assured by nearly everyone, they're all having a blast making *Sorority Row*.

Now, some readers are groaning, others scratching their heads. "Another remake? And of *The House on Sorority Row*? Why?" These are all valid questions. Even given Hollywood's fervor to redo so many of the '80s fave horror films, the mom-n-pop video store table *The House on Sorority Row* hardly seemed to be begging for the revamp treatment. Only hardcore slasher fans would recognize the title, and even they might be hard-pressed to recall the plot. Something about a prank gone wrong? It's OK—you're not alone in questioning this logic. But there was something about the premise that intrigued producer Mike Karz enough to option the rights to the film from previous writer/director Mark Rosman (who wrote the script "Seven Sisters" with Bobby Fine, and who is aboard the redux as executive producer), take it to the screenwriting team of Josh Stolberg and Pete Goldfinger (*Piranha 3D*) and pitch it to Summit Entertainment, which would soon become one of the most powerful studios in the country thanks to a little flick called *Twilight*.

I almost didn't accept the assignment. It's 2009 and Fangoria still owed me money for the set-visit I did the previous year, for *My Bloody Valentine 3-D*. Valentine had been...not quite a nightmare, but an unpleasant experience. The highlights were speaking with Patrick Lussier, the director who I'd admired, and the 3-D stereographer Max Penner, who showed me fresh-from-the-camera 3D effects on his cell phone. We were in a dank mine, none of the stars were on call that day, something that

annoyed my editor, Tony Timpone. Worst of all, for me at least, was that I had to "share" my visit time with a self-described "trust fund asshole" who worked as an online blogger for some now-defunct horror site. He also admitted to everyone who was in ear-shot, that his only reason for being there was to ask out Jamie King. He knew he didn't have a shot, said he, but he'd be damned if he didn't try. The rest of the time he spent trying to impress Lussier on his horror knowledge. He never asked a question, just interrupted the answers.

That Fango was delinquent was no fault of Tony's. Rest assured, I was in good company of the unpaid. I managed to get a personal guarantee of payment from Tony, though at a much lower rate, which suggested to

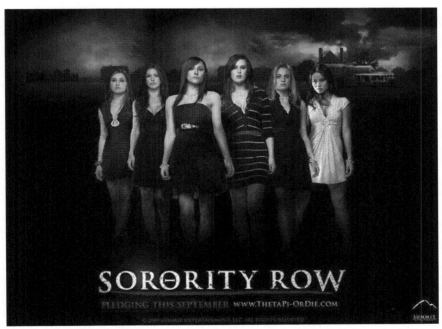

L-R: *Margot Harshman, Audrina Partridge, Briana Evigan, Rumer Willis, Leah Pipes, Jamie Chung. Copyright Summit Entertainment.*

13

me this marker was coming out of his own pocket and that alone was enough to get me to capitulate.

The Pittsburgh Film Office at the time was notoriously disorganized. They gave me the address of "an old warehouse" the production company had gutted to use for interior sets and the warning bells went off. "Oh, the Summit Building," I said. They hesitated, then said yes. We were talking at cross-purposes. The Crafton, PA, address was one I knew well: the old WRS Film and Video Lab where I spent three years working under hellish conditions as an optical printer. Jack Napor, owner and absconder of pension funds and health care payments, went quietly bankrupt, only for his one-time partner Russ Scheller to reopen the lab a year later as "Summit Film Laboratory." I was confusing one Summit for another. Summit the production company had moved into the now-abandoned Summit Laboratory, hence the momentary loss of bearings. It all came back as I walked past that fenced-in entry-way, the top looped with razor wire, looking for all the world like the entrance to a prison camp. Very appropriate given the atmosphere we all there once labored under. OSHA violations daily. We all lived in a cloud of processing chemicals, but were never issued masks or even latex gloves. Unless OSHA was on property, of course, in which case, the protective gear not only appeared, but was now mandatory.

This was the last week of production. The team had already shot their exteriors in Munhall, and a big graduation ceremony outside of Soldiers and Sailors Hall in Oakland.

Pittsburgh natives would once again get to play spot-the-landmark as we had with **Silence of the Lambs** and **Striking Distance**. Oddly enough, it was during **Striking Distance** where my wife first met Rumer Willis, who was the tender age of five. She and Demi Moore and a dozen of their closest bodyguards stopped in the grocery store of Amy's employ. I relayed this story to Willis later that day. She laughed. "That's hilarious. Tell her I said hi."

According to Karz, it wasn't the 1983 film that intrigued him so much as the timing. "I watched the original and thought it was a great basis for a remake," he recalls. "I suspected the horror genre would evolve away from the hardness and brutality [that was popular at that point], which I really believe was a reflection of the times— the war in Iraq; Hollywood was just responding to that. I suspected that over the next couple of years, as most genres do, it would go back to something that came before, like Scream. And Josh Stolberg knows everything there is to know about horror movies. I asked him if he knew House, and he said that it was more than ready for a remake, let's do it. So we started developing it, and our goal was to appeal to the fans of the original, but really play up the story, which is [about] people who make wrong decisions that come back to haunt them."

Jettisoning the majority of the previous film's plot, Stolberg and Goldfinger crafted a story about six coeds who decide to teach a philandering boyfriend a lesson. The prank goes badly, and one of

14

the sorority sisters, Megan (played by *The Hills'* Audrina Patridge), winds up dead. The group's self-styled "Queen Bee," Jessica (Leah Pipes from *Fingerprints*), bullies the rest into taking the classic vow of silence, and the girls toss Megan's body down a mineshaft, turn their backs on the scene of the crime and return to their house, thinking they can get on with their lives. Which, of course, they can't. Not just due to guilty consciences, but also, naturally, because of a vengeful mystery killer out to snuff the sorority. Karz, Stolberg and Goldfinger developed the script over a nearly three-year period, and then Karz saw an opportunity coming.

"We had just finished the script and I waited for [the update of *Prom Night*] to come out, suspected that it would do well and it did. We went out with our script the [following] Monday, and the studio that was most passionate about it was Summit. The head of production was Erik Feig, who had produced *I Know What You Did Last Summer* and was looking to bring back the genre in that style So we went with them, and five and a half months later, we were shooting."

Feig contacted Hendler, who at that time had only the Josh Holloway-starring chiller *Whisper*, which got dumped to DVD by Universal, on his feature resume. "Once you do a certain type of movie, everyone sends you scripts in that same genre," he notes. "I read a ton of genre screenplays, and it's really hard to find good ones. When this was sent to me, I saw the title and was like, 'Okaaay... might not be the best thing.' But I picked it up and as I read it, I said,

'Is this what I think it is? Is this a really sarcastic, funny, gory movie or is this a kind of sensationalized story about a bunch of girls running around getting killed?' You could interpret the script both ways. So I just went into the studio expecting that I'd say what I thought, rind if they hated me, then it just wasn't meant to be. I told them, 'I kinda think this is Mean Girls meets Scream.' And they were like, 'That's exactly what we want to do.'

"One of the things I loved so much about the script was that there is character development," Hendler continues. "I don't care if somebody dies if I don't know them, no matter how creative the death scene is. But if you like someone, you get scared for them. I went to the studio and said, 'There's a little character development here, and I'd like to take it further. Are

you cool with that?' So my first pass was primarily adding that. Usually they tell you, 'No, why don't you do a rewrite to put more blood in?' So it was refreshing. The more I got into it, the more fascinated I became with sorority culture: very prim and proper during the day and then very hedonistic nutzoness by night. On the one hand, sororities were founded for all the right reasons: preparing women for their lives, teaching sisterhood and all those values. But today, even those within would admit that it's very alcohol-fueled and does as much harm as good to girls. There are two sides to that coin, and by the end, we see which ones actually understand the meanings of those values. So it's a morality tale."

I was lucky enough to be on a pyro day as well as one set aside for effects pick-ups. It meant I'd get to hang out with Gino Crognale (who most know contemporaneously as the spiky zombie from The Walking Dead, the one kept as a pet by Pollyanna MacIntosh). I'd been introduced to Gino years ago via Robert Kurtzman. When I do set visits I always hang with the effects guys. They're the rock stars as far as I'm concerned. I waited until they reset the scene for the Molotov Cocktail. Surprisingly, D'Amore is on set and in the path of the bottle, fleeing seconds before it crashes into the wall. There are safety people all over the place. The bottle is candy glass, so her bare feet are in no danger. I probably will not witness a Vic Morrow incident today. But during the reset, I meet Hendler, who is about ten years younger than me in every way possible.

There's a slight delay as the crew resets for another scene involving fire, and Hendler shrugs. "Stunts are slow, and apparently it's bad manners to run onto the set screaming, 'Hurry the f**k up!'" he laughs. "Yesterday was slow too. Yesterday was the scene with Carrie Fisher blowing the hell out of the kitchen with a shotgun. Obviously, we couldn't blow stuff up with her in the room. So we got shots of her firing the blanks, then we turned around, set up these big sheets of plexiglass to protect the cameras—which were on computerized heads because we had to move everyone out of the room—then we blew up a bunch of stuff. Then we went crazy, because something didn't blow on the first take."

The director is a few years shy of 30, and didn't grow up with quite the same Star Wars fanaticism that so many of Fango's readers have. He doesn't quite feel the gravity of the fact that he gave Princess Leia a shotgun (!).

His actual response to my "How cool was it to see Princess Leia blasting a shotgun?" was: "Never saw it. A lot of the crew wouldn't leave her alone about it, though. I like to put a stop to that kind of shit." It turned me off of him immediately. He irritated me further by griping that the movie had "such a low budget," referring to the more than $12 million he'd been given to play with. My last film had cost $7,000. But then I didn't go to USC.

I'd missed Carrie Fisher by a day. That was heartbreaking.

Retroactively, I was sad to have missed Margo Harshman by the same number of days. I like her in everything

Carrie Fisher as "Mrs. Crenshaw". Princess Leia gets a shotgun. Not that it means much to Stewart Hendler. Photo copyright Summit Entertainment. All Rights Reserved.

I see her in. Plus, she was Fozzie Bear's original girlfriend on the pilot for The Muppets TV series. She was replaced by Riki Lindholme for the series, which also led to conflicting feelings. I like seeing Riki get work too.

When it came to casting, a net was thrown to find actresses who were not only beautiful, but could truly act and carry an unusual amount of weight on their shoulders, particularly for what may strike most observers at first as "just" a fright flick. Eventually, in addition to Pipes and Patridge, a host of lovely ladies was found including Briana Evigan (from *Fear Itself*'s "New Years Day"), Rumer Willis and Margo Harshman (both previously seen in *From Within*), Jamie Chung and, as the gun-toting housemother, Carrie Fisher. For the women in the audience, the film

provides Matt (*Death Sentence,* but more importantly, he was "The Brain" in Rian Johnson's *Brick*) O'Leary and Julian (*Donkey Punch*) Morris, but truthfully, this movie belongs to the leading ladies.

Not that there wasn't some trepidation at first. (After all, Patridge stars on *The Hills,* one of the bitchiest shows on television.) Evigan, daughter of former TV hunk Greg, plays Cassidy, the sisters' moral compass, and was the first to state what all the other cast members would confide later. "I was a little scared at first about getting along with so many females," she recalls. "All of us have said that to each other. It's no secret. But I don't think the cast could be more perfect."

Pipes echoes the sentiment. "There is none of that catty sorority bullshit [during shooting] that you see in the script. Usually when you get a bunch of girls on a set, you'll see some of

17

that, but we completely avoided it here. Luckily, we've had a week of rehearsal before filming, and during that time we all really did become like sorority sisters. We truly bonded. And the girls in this film are the most amazing ones I've ever met. I'm proud of all of us for coming together and carrying a movie on our shoulders as five young actresses. I don't know how many times I'm going to be able to have this experience, where I'm on a set with all leading ladies and really enjoying myself." And despite a story centered on sorority sisters, the cast wants to promise right now that you're not getting two-dimensional stereotypes this time around. "Everybody's role grew after it was cast," says Evigan. "When we first

read it, everyone thought, 'OK, you're the typical nice girl, you're the typical bitch, you're the drunk girl.' But each one of us really made [her part] her own, and worked to make you like each one."

Willis, she of the famous mom and dad, plays Ellie, whom she describes as Cassidy's sidekick. She too was lured in by the surprisingly complex script. "With horror movies, sometimes it's just about the gore, and the characters and story get lost. Or if it doesn't have as many effects, it gets a little bogged down and is not as scary. I liked that this has some great effects that were a thrill to watch being done. I mean, as scary as a girl crawling through a TV [in The Ring] can be, you watch it and go, 'OK, that's cool,

Nenhum segredo é para sempre.

PACTO SECRETO

but it won't happen to me.' With something like this, you watch and go, 'That could happen to anybody.' Situations can actually get out of hand. I know a number of stories about sororities and hazing where someone died because they actually did [a prank that went wrong] . So I enjoyed that element of the story."

And after her bloodsoaked turn in *From Within* , Willis is no stranger to gore. "I am a big fan of horror movies. It's always so much more fun when you get to be gruesome rather than pretty."

Morris, the token testosterone of today's on-set cast, falls right in step with his Gyno-American co-stars. "This one has deft characterization, stunning death sequences, a dark, twisted vein of humor—it's brilliant!" says the British actor, who came direct from promoting the Tom Cruise war epic *Valkyrie* to join *Sorority Row* as Cassidy's wannabe paramour, Andy. After the explosions and Nazi nastiness of the former, he becomes a bit philosophical about the differences in onscreen violence. "I'm a horror fan," Morris continues. "I want to see the blood. I love that. But in something like *Valkyrie*, the blood is very representational of something real, and you probably shouldn't enjoy it. In *Donkey Punch*, the premise also revolved around a prank gone wrong, and it's just devastating; there's no reprieve. Whereas that film treated it in a very dark, natural way, in something like this, it's free range—go ahead and enjoy it. It sounds sick, maybe, I know, but you should enjoy it. It's supposed to be fun. It's context—I don't know. It sounds horrible to say."

Without egotistical catfights, the biggest challenge for the cast was surviving the notoriously bipolar Pittsburgh autumn climate. First, Karz's perspective: "So far, shooting down here has been great. At first we were really freaked out about the weather. We're shooting in October, but it's set in spring. But we really got lucky. On our last day of exteriors, it was supposed to be sunny and it stayed sunny for about six hours, and just as we finished, it started to pour."

Now from Pipes: "It's very cold here in Pittsburgh." Indeed, she speaks to Fango in the soundstage hallway, bundled in a heavy jacket and gloves. "And we're all in very scanty outfits. Being practically naked in 27-degree weather in the middle of the night has been challenging. We like to say, 'We're Marines!' On those cold nights, we just said, 'If a Marine can do it, so can we! Let's go, ladies!' We got through it, and I'm really proud of us." D'Amore seems to take it more in stride—half Marine, half supermodel: "Well, a movie with a bunch of girls, odds are we're not going to be wearing much. I actually wear the least, because I get caught in bed with somebody and then I spend the rest of the movie in that little outfit. I don't have time [to throw on clothes] being chased by a killer. I don't really mind that, though, because I used to model and I was always in...those things," she says with a laugh—though she is also bundled inside a thick robe, waiting for her next shot.

When it was time to do the sit-downs with the actors, always between takes, things started to get even weirder. Not with the actors themselves; they were perfectly pleasant. I think I got along best with Pipes because we connected over adult things. She was irritated about a 401(k) she'd just opened and I'd just gone through something similar. So while all around us were screams and production, we were going through the vagaries of adulthood. I'd actually mistaken her as the oldest actress of the cast but she was actually at least a year or two behind the others. The girl I thought still in her teens was D'Amore, but she was the furthest into her twenties at that point. Pipes just struck me as more mature, possibly due to the boring finance conversation.

Already feeling the awful karma from returning to the former WRS, I'm now surrounded by young women in various stages of undress, all shivering in the unheated building. The publicist, David Linck, a perfect gentleman. But this odd woman who was hovering around him—I don't know that I ever knew her function, an assistant to someone, possibly an assistant director (my notes from this day are long gone), kept up a stream of inappropriate remarks, like some sort of entrapment tourettes. "Aren't you lucky to be here on a lingerie day?" she said to me upon shaking my hand. And "get ready to fall in love," as I was introduced to Evigan. At this point, I'm pushing forty, I'm devoutly married, all of these women look like children to me. Take the unprofessional angle out of it and you have a woman who seems like she's running a white slavery ring on the side and she's trying to feel me out as if I might be an oil sheik on the side. The only one she didn't make some sort of lewd comment about was Willis. "Don't ask her about her family," this woman told me, referring to Rumer's royal parentage.

"Are they in the movie?" I ask her. She shakes her head no. "Then why would I bring them up?" We didn't talk much after that.

Every film set is surreal—you follow cables snaking behind plain wooden walls, turn a comer and suddenly you're in a completely furnished and very elegant elegant living room (albeit littered with plastic cups and prop alcohol bottles that all indicate "sorority party"). For this reporter, there is an added element of strange, because the last time he had set foot inside the massive building at 100 Napor Drive, in the heart of Crafton, PA, he was an employee of WRS Film and Video Lab. Where there is now a spiral staircase and a chandelier, there once was a long bank of videotape machines, spooling endless public-domain cartoons onto cheap VHS tapes. Where FX genius Gino Crognale is prepping a new and gruesome Sorority Row gag, there used to be a temperature controlled glass vault containing a maze of shelves holding cans of original negatives of such films as Orson Welles' *Othello*, *The Pit and the Pendulum* and George A. Romero's *Night of the Living Dead* (with decaying labels reading "Night of the Anubis").

It's been almost twenty years since I last worked at WRS. To this day I still get calls from filmmakers asking me if I knew what became of all of those films that we'd had stored away

in our vault. Othello I was able to help rescue, but as far as I could ever ascertain, half of the vault's contents left unclaimed—Jack was sued constantly for basically holding prints hostage for "storage fees"—was moved to an Iron Mountain facility. The rest was likely dumped. Because that was the respect that man had for both people and product.

Where the interior set stood— with its spiral staircase and hanging lit chandelier—had once been the tape loading area. Damp despite atmosphere control, the room was once floor to ceiling with VHS machines running tape off spools directly to cutters, loaded from there onto the plastic cassettes. I worked that section a couple of times when work in the film department had slowed to a crawl. It was miserable. You're on your feet all day, blasted by the noise of three dozen spinning, droning machines. Your fellow co-workers are all on work-release from one of the local prisons. They hugged the walls when they passed you in the hallway. They always stared at their feet. They weren't supposed to be on the grounds after 10pm, but I'd worked enough late shifts to see the same faces, well after midnight. Small talk was discouraged, and that was likely a blessing. One of the guys in that section had smashed in a supervisor's car windows because he couldn't use comp time for "when I was in jail!"

An additional fact has made things slightly creepier for the cast, already immersed in their world of sorority-girl mortality: The WRS building was a meatpacking plant during the early part of the 20th century, complete with slaughterhouse. Just outside the rear doors to the stage is a twin set of rails on which coal carts would be loaded with discarded animal innards, to be trucked out for incineration or delivery to dog-food companies.

"I knew it!" Evigan says. "It has been the big mystery—no one was sure. We thought it might be an old school, because of the hallway tile, but then we'd come back here and see drains in the floor. That's just..." She doesn't finish the sentence, but smiles and shudders—even bundled up inside the heated "warming tent."

Apparently Evigan and Pipes had "slaughterhouse" in some sort of informal betting pool. One of the other girls was convinced it had been a Depression-era hospital, which wasn't a bad guess considering the age of the neighborhood. Most of Pittsburgh's lower-class neighborhoods were either Company Store row houses or other such remnants of the once dominant steel industry. I was happy to have brought them a sense of closure. I don't think anyone felt better after the confirmation.

After meeting Evigan, lunch was served. It was then I witnessed first hand what a $12M budget buys you. The craft services spread was bigger than most Las Vegas buffets. There were two steak stations. There was a table piled with nothing but baked goods and cakes. One was nothing but salads. This wasn't blue collar picnic food either. These all came from an on-set chef. But considering that the majority of the crew were either former or current models, only the salad table looked like road kill. Most of the meat went uneaten, likely tossed at the end of the day. I have a thing about not eating on sets I'm not *actively working, but David convinced me to pile on a plate. I sat with him and a couple of the grips I knew from when they'd worked on **our** sets. A lot of guys in the Pittsburgh grip union at the time got their first start with us. Any time I run into Don Yockey, who'd studied effects under my partner Bill Homan, I ask him how things are going on whatever "show" he's working on. "Worst shoot ever," he says, without fail. "Fucking ridiculous." Pittsburgh grips are never happy, but they're always entertaining.*

Crognale, around the corner, is prepping what will be one of the movie's signature kills. We won't spoil it here, but even just a few feet away, this reporter is disturbed by what he sees. The KNB EFX veteran grins, talking as he works. "I'm exhausted, man, but thrilled!" he says. "I flew completely alone on this one. It was crazy. When [producer Bill Bannerman] approached me, because I had done *Shelter* [a Julianne Moore-starring chiller also shot in Pittsburgh] with him earlier in the year, he said, 'This seems like something you can handle on your own.' I said, 'I'm totally game for it.' And as we began, it didn't seem like much, but as we got moving into it, I'd get a phone call saying, 'Hey, we're gonna hit this guy in the head with an ax, so can you build us a fake head?' Things just kept getting added on and added on. I'd race out to Bob [Kurtzman's company Precinct 13 in Ohio] to run molds, rash back. By the end, I'll have done about a dozen different gags. That's a fair amount of stuff."

The big question must be asked, and his grin widens. "Oh, yeah—we're going for an R," he says. "Originally, they wanted a PG-13, but no—Bill said, 'We got the R. Everything you're working on, go bigger!' In the ax-to-the-head gag, the blood just flowed! It was heavy duty, like a waterfall."

The effect alluded to above, the one I couldn't disclose, was for Harshman's death scene. Her character is a barely functioning alcoholic—nicknamed "Chugs" in the film—who goes to her shrink intending to bone him for an oxy prescription. She lies down on a lounge, drinking deep from a wine bottle. The killer sneaks up and jams it into her mouth. Blood sprays up into the bottle, mixing with the alcohol. Harshman's throat bulges as the bottle neck invades her.

They'd shot the live work in an off-site set. Harshman had already wrapped. Gino had prepped an upper-torso puppet of Harshman that could take the abusive bottle without complaint. "I broke the first goddamned bottle on the first take," Gino said. "We got one good one but I'm trying to convince them to do a third to really nail it." I think he got what he wanted. The effect was horrific to witness in person and it's just as effective in the film. Effects guys are rock stars.

The prep work is drawing to a close, though. His AD nods that they'll be ready soon and that director of photography Ken (*Quarantine*) Seng is sending his camera guys out to change the magazine on the huge 35mm Panavision camera. "I'm a die-hard film fanatic," Hendler says. "Stylistically, Ken is awesome. We both wanted to do something different—handheld, a little more verite to make it feel like you're standing in the room. *Children of Men* is a good reference—so much of it is handheld, but everything's gorgeous. It's like, 'Oh, we accidentally got the most beautiful frame ever!' So it's very controlled. That's a blessing."

*As off-putting as Hendler's words are, his enthusiasm is contagious. My ultimate reward for all of this came a few months later when the film was finally released. My Bloody Valentine 3D is such a cock-up of a film, structurally and script-wise, it was a let down and a disappointment. Sometimes a lousy set visit can be erased if the movie is good. For **Sorority Row**, nothing was specifically unpleasant, but everything was definitely off. The atmosphere of "girl power" jammed up against the demands of exploitation was clearly a tug of war battled both on set and in film. **Sorority Row** ended up being a pretty solid movie, and it's ultimate feminism is in the murky motivation of the male villain. The idea that the sins of the past can be kept covered by a series of murders has never been anything new, and his motivations to "protect" the woman he loves, by committing ridiculously- meticulous killings with a tricked-out tire iron is silly at best, and is meant to be the product of toxic masculinity writ large within an otherwise weak- willed character. The women keep to their pledge of sisterhood and secrecy, and it's*

a bond that frustrates but you can grow to understand it. In the film, the boyfriends are all ciphers, barely existing in this dimension. The women are all well-drawn, flawed individuals. You don't always understand their motivations because they're all caught up, very realistically, in an unreal situation. The motive of the killer is as much an afterthought as his costume: that plain black robe meant to evoke vague dread, the weapon more important, more iconic.

As the fire department goes over a safety checklist with the stunt crew, Hendler sums up the film, smiling: "It's a pro-Communist film with anti-Semitic overtones," he laughs. "I want people to walk away from a fun ride. It's not meant to be anything too cranial. It's supposed to be old-fashioned, thrilling with some laughs.

Above: Briana Evigan as "Cassidy".

23

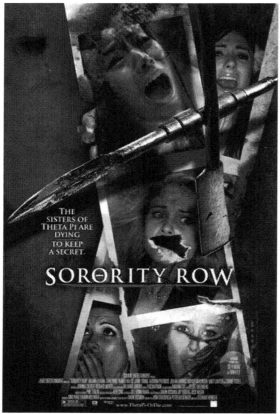

THE
SISTERS OF
THETA PI ARE
DYING
TO KEEP
A SECRET.

SORORITY ROW

www.ThetaPiOnThe.com

as if it's one of your own. Unless you're of the breed of journo where you have to tear down the thing you covered out of some sense of fairness, or because you felt personally betrayed by a substandard product after you'd dedicated your time to its promotion. Journalists are human too. We're irrational and get just as drunk on tinctures of power like anyone else. There was talk of a sequel but it never went anywhere.

Summit Films was bought out by Lionsgate in 2012. The last thing I'd heard Hendler was connected with was the **Max Steele** movie based on the action figure line. Apparently his **Halo** web series was a big hit. I hope he's well.

Evigan, Pipes, D'Amore, Willis, they all seem to be doing well for themselves. There was a lot of buzz about Morris for the longest time and he thought **Valkyrie** was going to lead to mega-stardom. He didn't say that in so many words, but there was hope in his voice. He does a lot of TV, a lot of shows I don't watch, but success is success is success.

I hope there's a little something for everyone in this. And [Fango readers] are f**king awesome. Nowadays, it's such an interactive process, making a movie.

There has been a bit of a buzz on-line and you read what people say, and it definitely informs what we do. We listen! We're all reading the boards." Picture goes up, and Hendler goes back to work. More sorority girls are put in peril, and the WRS demons retreat into the shadows.

Sorority Row was released to respectable returns in 2009 and it was a surprisingly solid movie. Again, that was a relief. When you cover a film, you become possessive of it,

The last time I was anywhere near WRS, the weeds had overtaken the parking lot, but the barbed wire still topped the fence. Had Shirley Jackson visited it, she'd have written "The Lab on Haunted Hill." Some labs are just born evil.

script-ozoology: Life Imitating Art

BY BILL ADCOCK

Illustrations by Bill Hahner

I hate to break it to you but cryptozoology is all bullshit. [*The opinions expressed in this article and by the writer in real life do not necessarily reflect those of Exploitation Nation.*] No one is ever actually going to find Bigfoot hanging around western Canada (or Texarkana, for that matter), the biggest thing you're going to find in Loch Ness is a kind of fish called a sturgeon, and there are no relic dinosaurs wandering around the central African jungle. Everything can be boiled down to misidentification of known animals, mirages, wishful thinking, and people pulling pranks. Actually, a lot of it is just people pulling pranks. Oddly enough (or perhaps not oddly at all), movies play a significant role in influencing what we see when we see monsters in the wild. Just as the creatures sought by cryptozoologists are referred to as "cryptids," we might well call those based on Hollywood fantasy "Scriptids."

With all due respects to those cryptozoologists who do take their research and investigations seriously, many members of that breed (and this is true of UFO researchers as well) are an intellectually lazy bunch, content to recite claims from second- and third-hand sources without taking the time to look deeper. [*See above*] It is the skeptic researchers (again, not to be confused with the contingent of "armchair debunkers") who often turn up the information that the cryptozoologists should have had in hand in the first place.

El Chupacabra

We will begin with one of the newest superstars of cryptozoology, having only appeared on the scene in 1995. The Chupacabra, or goat-sucker, is an alleged mystery creature that preys on livestock, draining blood through (depending on the version of the story you hear) one, two or three

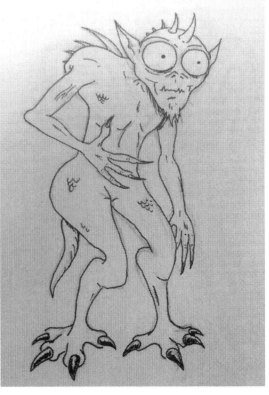

holes in the victim's neck. First seen in Puerto Rico, reports of the creature have spread through Latin America and the American southwest.

While recent reports have conflated the Chupacabra with a steady stream of mangy coyotes in Texas, the original description given by Madelyne Tolentino of Puerto Rico describes a much different beast – four feet tall, green-skinned, resembling an alien with sharp claws and a row of bony spines down its back, possibly the creation of the US government via genetic engineering—maybe using alien DNA. The Tolentino sighting was the first reported encounter with a Chupacabra, and set the template for subsequent sightings by other witnesses. Once Tolentino's account was publicized, it resulting in a flurry of reported sightings, creating the impression that populations of Chupacabras had exploded out from Puerto Rico in all directions.

The Chupacabra was not the only green, alien creature with a row of bony spines down its back that owed its existence to a US government-backed genetics lab to arrive in 1995. Preceding the Chupacabra was Sil, Natasha Henstridge's character from the film *Species*.

In his 2011 book *Tracking the Chupacabra*, skeptical researcher Benjamin Radford documents his five-year investigation into the origins of the Chupacabra phenomenon. While interviewing Tolentino about her sighting, Radford discovered that she had not only gone to see the film just a few days before her sighting took place, but believed the film to be a fictionalization of events actually going on at government sites in Puerto Rico. Tolentino even offered the opinion that the creature Sil from the film was modeled after the creature she saw a few days later. Which is a more believable option – that a woman with a perhaps fantasy prone personality "saw" a creature in real life that she'd seen in the theater less than a week before, or that she really saw a previously undocumented creature, possibly of extraterrestrial origin, that coincidentally resembled the creature from the film? Ockham's Razor suggests the former.

With the original, primary sighting of the creature so likely to have been based on a B-horror movie that Ben Kingsley bizarrely agreed to be in, what are we to make of subsequent sightings? Tolentino having essentially seen Natasha Henstridge certainly weakens the likelihood of such a creature as the Chupacabra in its original form existing; perhaps this is why recent US sightings have consisted of the "Chupacabra" name being applied to coyotes that have lost their fur to sarcoptic mange. As for the "flap" of sightings in the mid- to late-1990s, the most likely explanation lies in psychology; with the Tolentino report being publicized so widely and so aggressively, especially among Hispanic communities, people were essentially being "primed" to see the creature, their brains filling in details and convincing themselves of sightings, which is a common trend with these sorts of paranormal events.

And all those goats and chickens mysteriously drained of blood...? Well, when an actual pathologist examined the carcasses, it was found that the bite marks matched those of feral dogs (a common pest in Puerto

Rico) and that the carcasses were in fact…not drained of blood, after all. They still had plenty of blood in them, in fact.

Nessie

Yes, the venerable and respected Loch Ness Monster may be a child of Hollywood. Some will trace sightings of "Nessie" to the 7th century text *Vita Columbae*, a biography of St. Columba written and sent to Rome as part of the canonization process. In this text, St. Columba is reported to have come across a group of men burying the victim of a monster attack. Proceeding on, he arrives at the River Ness (which flows out of Loch Ness) where he sees a monster about to attack a swimmer. Making the sign of the Cross, Columba ordered the creature away, causing it to flee (and causing the witnesses of this event to immediately convert to Christianity).

Two problems with this. First, the *Vita Columbae* is one big collection of miracles performed by Columba, because it was being sent to Rome to petition for him to be made a saint. Other passages have him dispelling storms with a wave of his hand, stopping floods, restoring withered crops and bringing the dead back to life. It's inherently a piece of propaganda. Second, there's nothing to tie this creature to what we now thing of as the Loch Ness Monster. More likely, the "River Ness Monster" is a Kelpie, a traditional Scottish water monster that drowned and ate those who strayed too close to the water. More on Kelpies in a moment.

We then have a gap in the Loch Ness Monster's record. It doesn't show up again until 1933. I discount the Mackenzie sighting dated to 1871 or '72, because he never thought to report his sighting until 1934, making its veracity dubious and more likely to be him attempting to cash in on the interest in a monster with his own back-dated tale.

The uptick in sightings in 1933 is frequently attributed to the construction of a new road along the edge of the Loch, making the water more visible and, in theory, disturbing the monster and causing it to surface more frequently to see what was causing the disturbance. But there was another incident in 1933 that may have influenced the first "modern" sightings –the release of the original *King Kong*.

In August 1933, George Spicer reported seeing a large, gray-skinned creature, bulky and round with a long, thin neck ending in a smallish head, without visible limbs, cross the road in front of his car and dive into the Loch. This creature had a "lamb or other small animal" in its jaws.

As researchers Dr. Donald Prothero and Daniel Loxton noted in their 2013 book *Abominable Science*, a very similar image appears in 1933's *King Kong*; Carl Denham and his crew, in pursuit of Kong, are forced to cross a lake on a raft. A Brontosaurus surfaces (at the time, it was believed that sauropods, the family of long-necked dinosaurs, were too heavy to walk on hand and instead wallowed in swamps to support their weight) and capsizes the raft before pursuing the men on to dry land. At least one man is picked up in the Brontosaurus' mouth and shaken violently before being discarded; in the enormous creature's grip, the man looks very much like a "small animal". The way the Brontosaurus moves across the screen during the pursuit, its legs obscured by foliage, mirrors the way the "monster" moves in Spicer's story, seemingly without legs. Damningly, in an interview a few months after his sighting, the interviewer mentioned this scene to Spicer, who replied that he had seen the film, and agreed that the creature he saw was very similar to the one in the film.

What Spicer may have actually seen was a large seal crossing the road (seals are a frequent sight around Loch Ness, coming down the River Ness from the north sea, and likely account for a number of sightings) in poor light and while tired; their brain "filled in" details from the Brontosaurus. This is not unusual or unheard of; it's just how the human brain works. But it has troubling implications for Nessie.

You see, Spicer's account is the first in which the monster has a long neck. It is the progenitor of all subsequent accounts in which the monster is described as having a long, flexible neck. And if the first account can be explained away as tired eyes and memories of a monster movie, what does that do to all those subsequent accounts?

More likely than not, Loch Ness ended up with a "lake monster" because for generations folklore had attributed it as being a home of kelpies, the mythical water monsters of Celtic myth; and before one suggests that kelpies were inspired by sightings of a lake monster, please keep in mind that the kelpies were demonic, shapeshifting horses, capable of disguising themselves as naked women, who lured children into the water to eat. Not a whole lot

of similarity there, but they do create something of a preexisting inclination to the idea that Loch Ness is a home to monsters.

With increased secularization in the 20th century, the demonic horses became passé, and the imagery of the mighty dinosaur got mapped onto the generic "water monster" in its place. Kind of like how "getting kidnapped by fairies" evolved into "abducted by aliens."

Bigfoot

Bigfoot. Sasquatch. The Big "B." Mr. Foot. Yeah, he's not real either. Hate to break it to you, but most Bigfoot sightings are either hoaxes and pranks, or bears seen in poor lighting conditions. Mapping all recorded Bigfoot sightings reveals that all of them are within the known range of the American Brown Bear.

"Bigfoot" entered the American public consciousness in 1958 when Jerry Crew, a construction worker in northern California, reported giant, barefoot human footprints around a bulldozer on a site. "Bigfoot" visited the site several times, leaving tracks but nothing more. Crew's boss, Ray Wallace, was well known for his love of practical jokes, and in 2002 his family revealed that Wallace had carved a pair of big wooden feet, strapped them over his boots, and gone stomping through the mud in 1958.

Movies come into the Bigfoot picture first in 1967. Roger Patterson, a California con-man and prankster, decided he wanted to make a movie about Bigfoot, got a camera, even ordered and modified a gorilla suit to serve as his monster. But then, Patterson got a better idea. If people would pay to see a Bigfoot movie, he reasoned, they might pay a lot more to see footage of a real, live Bigfoot. And heck, he already had the costume.

So Patterson and his friend Bob Gimlin got on their horses, loaded the camera and went out "Bigfoot hunting," and wouldn't you know, Bigfoot—specifically, a female Bigfoot with enormous, furry breasts — walks right in front of the camera. What a coincidence!

The grainy, shaky piece of footage that would become known as the Patterson-Gimlin footage has been held up by Bigfoot believers as the single best piece of evidence for the existence of Bigfoot since 1968. Kind of funny, isn't it, how nothing better than this has come along in almost fifty years.

While based on artwork that had appeared in men's adventure magazines for almost a decade prior, Patterson's busty

Sasquatchette became a template for all future sightings—a defining image of what "Bigfoot" looked like. Reports of Bigfeet with extra-long arms, hunched posture or rounded heads quickly died off (for the most part; Texarkana's "Beast of Boggy Creek" seems to have retained its chimpanzee-like proportions), replaced by tall, straight-backed creatures with conical heads and human-like proportions.

Twenty years later, the suit designed by Rick Baker for the film

Harry and the Hendersons would prove even more defining of what "Bigfoot" was. A number of prominent cryptozoologists have expressed their dislike of the film on the grounds that it has proven so influential that witnesses are filling in details from the suit when filing reports of sightings.

Memory is a weird, tricky thing, prone to exaggeration. While a witness might initially report just seeing a large, dark figure moving away from them in the woods, future recounting might define the color, the shape of the head, limbs, etc. And reports that have been filed over the last thirty years, if sorted by head shape, fur color, etc., show that overwhelmingly people are reporting a creature that looks *exactly* like Harry. Reports of blonde, gray, or black-furred Bigfeet have dropped off to almost nil, as have reports of Bigfeet greater than eight feet tall or less than seven. The snarling, savage Bigfoot of the beef jerky commercials is now an anomaly – people prefer to see a placid-faced, cuddly Bigfoot that will sneak up to your porch and take the blueberry muffin you left out for him.

John Lithgow changed the way you see Bigfoot. Let that sink in a minute.

I could continue on but I think this is a good place to conclude this discussion, at least for now. I think the point has been demonstrated that pop culture influences our perception of "real life" monsters just as much as they influence the pop culture we consume. It might be difficult to accept that they're not real – that they're not out waiting to be discovered in the forests of British Columbia or some deep Scottish lake. Instead they're a part of us, a deep-rooted part of our collective psyche as a species, a scratching at some primeval itch, some need for monsters that we all have. And honestly, I think that's even more fascinating than a relic dinosaur or anachronistic ape-man could ever be.

[*Again, this is all Bill. Do not leave flaming bags of animal droppings on our porch.*]

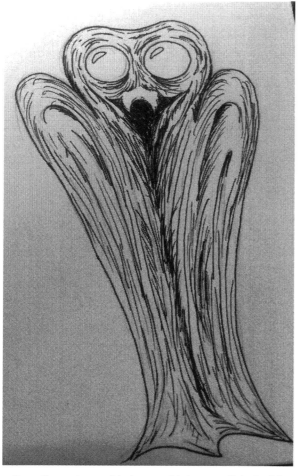

Above: Bonus picture of the happiest Mothman in all the land, by Bill Hahner.

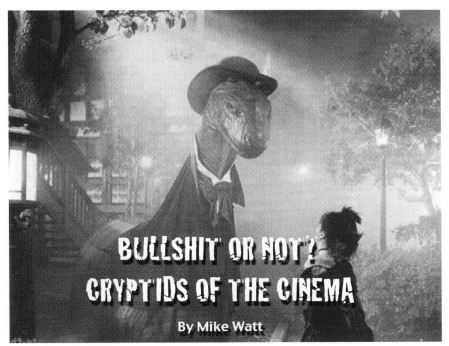

BULLSHIT OR NOT?
CRYPTIDS OF THE CINEMA

By Mike Watt

In terms of things I care about the existence of *cryptids*—as crypto-zoologists apparently call the likes of skunk apes, Bigfoot, Yetis, Nessies, Mothmen, Jersey Devils, and antidisestablishmentarianists—ranks somewhere below my interest in paint swatches and natural rock formations that look like famous celebrities. Yes, I'm sure that paving stone you found in your back yard is the spitting image of F. Murray Abraham, but I'm not paying $50 for it on Ebay. Now, that being said, I really don't have any skin in the game when it comes to the veracity of these creatures' existence. I approach belief in *cryptids* the same way I approach belief in religious deities: I don't know for sure if they exist or not, so who am I to say, definitively, that they don't. And just as I don't particularly subscribe to any religious denomination (for the record, I'm a recovering Catholic and an agnostic with an option to buy), I

will not denigrate anyone's belief in such things. I've witnessed first-hand the comfort that faith brings to people in crisis, so if someone finds comfort in believing Bigfoot lives in their back yard, or their neighbors are harboring chupacabras to protect them from the government, who am I to question that comfort?

I could make the argument that with the invention of satellite photography, not to mention Google Maps—a traveling map-spy just passed by my house not an hour ago—you'd think we'd have definitive proof by now of mothman getting his mail, or at the very least someone would have gotten a selfie with Mounty the Montauk Monster by now. But the best we get are blurry photos, death-bed faking confessions, and odd audio recordings of things that could be a skunk ape mating call or could be a faulty garbage truck hydraulic. My point is, I can't say for sure these things don't exist. And not just because I've never seen a Sasquatch—I've never seen a live wombat or someone who voted for Gary Johnson, but that doesn't mean *those* don't exist. (But at the very least, I've seen pictures. Although I think the Gary Johnson voter was a fake.)

But at the same time, as my business partner and crypto-expert Bill Homan pointed out, "Gorillas didn't officially exist until 1902; Okapi in 1901; Coelacanth in 1938; Komodo Dragons in 1910; and Ghost Octopus in 2016. Every year new animals are discovered somewhere." And let's not forget that there are multiple species we thought were completely extinct that turn out to be merely endangered. Again, we can point to the coelacanth, that heartiest of fish no longer extinct, nor mythical. Let's look no further than the lizard called "Bocourt's terrific skink", also known, presumably by enemies of Bocourt, as "The Terror Skink", that only exists on the Île des Pins (Isle of Pines) off the coast of New Caledonia. First: just because it's remote doesn't mean it's extinct. Second, why doesn't "The Terror Skink" have its own movie yet?

So if you're a cryptophile, all power to you. You won't get snark from me about it. (Although, I will admit to an occasion where Amy Lynn Best and I were set up at a local horror convention and were next to a UFO-ologist who scoffed at our silly horror movies. "We concentrate on the *real* stuff," he said, shoving Project Blue Book literature into my hand while refusing my reciprocal offer of *Splatter Movie: The Director's Cut.* Not cool, "Truth is Out There" Dude.) While I might not understand the

fascination with the gentle wood apes, I don't have to understand it. Until the woods behind my house are thick with believers crashing about at all hours and asking to use my bathroom, I'm going to remain neutral on the subject. Although I will say I don't believe I have any Bigfeet in my locality, so please, don't ask to use my bathroom.

While we have the cinematic adventures of Bigfoot pretty well covered in the Review section, I thought I would take a few spare moments to address the lesser-famous of the cryptids and their own sporadic appearances.

The Mothman.

Until 2002, when Richard Gere descended on Kittanning, located just outside of Pittsburgh, I was blissfully unaware of the very legend of The Mothman, let alone his prophecies. Apparently, this creature was first sighted in 1966, in Point Pleasant, West Virginia. According to the *Point Pleasant Register,* dated Wednesday, November 16, 1966, two young men, Steve Mallette and Roger Scarberry, who insist they were not drinking[1] saw a, quote, "bird... or something," standing on or above a power station. "It definitely wasn't a flying saucer." It had wings, glowing eyes, and flew away "clumsey" [sic] at about 100 miles per hour.

Other sightings followed throughout 1966 and '67, and somewhere along the line, this thing was connected to the collapse of the Silver Bridge, traversing the Ohio River, on December 15, 1967. Though

---

[1] Hey, read the piece for yourself here: https://web.archive.org/web/20071011230219/http://www.westva.net/mothman/1966-11-16.htm)

official investigations released in 1971 determined that the cause of the collapse was stress corrosion in an eyebar in a suspension chain, the Mothman was definitely there to warn people of the impending doom. Obviously, this warning went unheeded, as 46 people were killed in the bridge collapse.

Still, this tenuous connection was enough to inspire journalist and famed UFOlogist, John Keel (who coined the phrase—and concept—of "The Men in Black"), to write *The Mothman Prophecies* in 1975, translating the tenuous into the definitive. This book inspired the 2002 film[2] of the same name and is the basis for most peoples' frame of reference for this silvery harbinger of doom. A moderate success, the film spawned countless imitations, all meant to subtract dedicated cryptozoologists from their hard-earned cash. While *The Mothman Prophecies* [see review] presents the creature as a neutral observer, possibly a harbinger, the majority of the following films give the cryptid a more malevolent personality. Some of these include:

Mothman (2010), was a SyFy original starring *Firefly*'s Jewel Staite, and is more a "young people in the woods" film, with the titular creature stalking and possibly causing the deaths of the cast.

Eyes of the Mothman (2011) is a three-hour documentary (!) about the creature and its various sitings. This was directed by Matthew J.

Pellowski, a horror producer and director currently attached to the zombie film *The Dead Rising.*

The Mothman Curse (2014) is set in a museum for budgetary reasons. It was directed by Richard Mansfield, who has directed and produced a number of impressive short films, including a creepy adaptation of the German nursery story, "Suck-A-Thumb". *Curse* has an interesting and moody trailer, but lots of 1-Star abuse on IMDB.

Moth (2016) is a Hungarian film that transplants the creature to the European countryside and, again, the creature causes more havoc than it prevents.

There are numerous documentaries extant on this particular creature, and

---

[2] An earlier film loosely based on the book, but shot on location in Point Pleasant, *Mothman*, was produced in 2000, written and directed by Douglas TenNapel, best-known as the producer of the subversive cartoon series, *Earthworm Jim.*

in most of which, "The Mothman" is credited as "Himself". There is no indication who his agent might be or what his day rate entails.

The Maryland Goatman.

I came across this entry while doing research for this very article and it is the very definition of a lazy person's urban legend. Dating back to 1971, best-remembered as an era with lackluster television, the military draft, and accessible marijuana, The Maryland Goatman is described as a half-man, half-goat creature, "carnivorous and axe-wielding (!)" According to cryptozologist Mark Opsasnick, "There were basically three aspects to the Goatman legend, as described by early newspaper accounts. Number one is that they described a creature that was half-man, half-animal, walking on two feet. The other aspect of the legend was that it was a mad scientist -- a scientist who worked in the Beltsville Agricultural Research Center who was experimenting on goats, and the experiment went astray, and he started attacking cars with an ax. [He'd attack] anyone who would roam the back roads of the Beltsville Agricultural Research Center. The third aspect of the legend was that it was just an old hermit who retreated to the woods and would be seen walking alone at night along Fletchertown Road, and when anyone would come around, he'd just run away."[3]

Sadly, The Goatman only received one cinematic tribute that I could find,

[3] Aratani, Lori, 2008. "The Keeper of Local Haunted Lore." Washington Post, October 26.http://www.washingtonpost.com/wp-dyn/content/article/2008/10/23/AR2008102303620.html

Jimmy Tupper vs. the Goatman of Bowie (2010), written, directed, and starring "YouTube Star" (which seems like another cryptid entry), Andrew Bowser.

Then there's the wonderfully named...

Pope Lick Monster.

Imagine my disappointment that this creature is not literal. The idea of slobber-covered pontiffs is just too delightful. "Over the past few decades, an urban legend has circulated in Louisville, Kentucky about a hideous goat-headed humanoid known as The Pope Lick Monster, whose unusual name is taken from Pope Lick Creek in the neighborhood of Fisherville, the site of a huge railroad trestle on

The Pope Lick Sheepman.
Photo copyright Germantown Films.
All Rights Reserved.

which the creature is said to dwell," reads the 2013 Fearnet article, "The Bizarre Legend of Louisville KY's 'Pope Lick Monster'," by Gregory Burkart (February 21, 2014)[4]. "Most accounts of the monster describe it as a nightmarish cross between man and goat (or sheep), with pale skin, ram's horns and thick, matted hair. But from there, the stories start to diverge – especially when it comes to the creature's method of attacking intruders. Some say it leaps from the trestle to pounce on people below; others claim it uses vampire-like hypnosis to lure victims onto the tracks; some tales even suggest it takes down its prey with a handy axe."

So we have another creature that isn't scary enough on its own, it has to use weapons. Ron Schildknecht wrote and directed the 1988 short film, *The Legend of the Pope Lick Monster*, shot on 16mm for just $6,000. The biggest controversy surrounding the film was concern by railroad officials that bored teenagers might start visiting the dilapidated trestle and might be injured. Schildknecht permitted Norfolk Southern Railroad an opportunity to warn people against imitating the dangers depicted in the film, particularly one "misleading" instance where a teen hangs from the trestle for more than seven minutes as a train goes by. This normally, say officials, leads to horrible death. If you look around, you can find *The Legend of the Pope Lick Monster* online.

The Jackalope.
Now here's a little lagomorph

4 https://web.archive.org/ web/20140609044915/ http://www.fearnet. com/news/news-article/bizarre-legend-louis- ville-kys-pope-lick-monster

that gets no respect. The Unofficial Mythological Creature of Wisconsin (legitimate legislation is frequently introduced into State government to upgrade the creature to "Official"—as early as 2015, a bill died in the Senate, but let's take a moment to marvel that it's made that far *at least a half dozen times*! Wisconsin doesn't even have gravity 24-hours a day!), the American Jackalope made its debut in the 1930s, when hunter/taxidermy enthusiast Douglas Herrick first grafted deer antlers onto a jackrabbit carcass and sold the monstrosity to a local hotel in Douglas, Wyoming. So popular were the alternatively-horny rabbits that a retail outlet in South Dakota contracted Herrick and his brother to mass produce them, thereby (possibly) leading to a mass murdering of jackrabbits throughout the Pacific Northwest (I have no proof of this).

Legends grew up around the antlered rabbit. Tales of hunters donning stovepipe shin guards to avoid ankle goring. The blood-chilling sound of the jackalope stalking its immortal enemy, the vampire carrot (again, I have no proof of this claim). I could go on. But does the Jackalope get his cinematic due? He does not. For years,

Jackalope Postcard, 1968 Dexter Press West Nyack, New York. All Rights Reserved.

he was mockingly voiced by Dave Coulier on *America's Funniest Home Videos*, a show whose problems can be traced back to the lies within the title. While it is frequently featured in kids' books, and you can hunt the silly things in *Red Dead Redemption*, the only full-fledged movie to feature the jackalope was a little mockumentary titled *Stag Bunny*, (2006), from executive producer Dustin Carpenter.

Still, the Stag Bunny can take consolation in the fact that it appears on Lottery Tickets and virtually every piece of state advertising in Wisconsin. And if you can make it there, you can make it anywhere.

The Flatwoods Monster.

West Virginia is either desperate for attention or there are monsters every ten feet throughout the state. First sighted in Flatwoods in Braxton County, West Virginia, on September 12, 1952, this flat-faced, red-eyed creature was accompanied by a bright light in the sky that many UFOlogists believe to be its originating craft. The three young boys who first saw the creature at the farm of one G. Bailey Fisher, as well as several others who also witnessed the creature, reportedly fell ill, their symptoms similar to exposure to mustard gas. Skeptics have claimed that what the boys witnessed was the crash of a meteor that may have released a biotoxin, or kicked up some sort of irritant upon impact that the bystanders inhaled. The creature itself, described as over 7 ft. tall, has been explained as "an owl".

A barn owl. A *big fucking barn owl*. An owl first described as "a towering 'man-like' figure with a round, red 'face' surrounded by a 'pointed, hood-

The Flatwoods Monster. Image taken from the "Villains Wikia". Artist Unknown.

like shape.' The body was dark and seemingly colorless, but some would later say it was green, and Mrs. May reported drape-like folds. The monster was observed only momentarily, as suddenly it emitted a hissing sound and glided toward the group. Lemon responded by screaming and dropping his flashlight, whereupon everyone fled."[5]

While creatures resembling what was described have shown up as bosses in video games like *The Legend of Zelda: Majora's Mask*, no full-length movie has yet been made, though according to the ever-reliable IMDB, there is a film in the works.

The Jersey Devil.

If you ever want to leap into a rabbit hole of history and hysteria, look no further than The Jersey Devil,

[5] "Jersey Devil and Folklore", Pinelands Preservation Alliance. http://www.pinelandsalliance.org/history/devil/

currently said to be running amok throughout the area of New Jersey known as the Pinelands. According to the Pineland Preservation Alliance website: "Designated in 1938 as the country's only state demon, the Jersey Devil is described as a kangaroo-like creature with the face of a horse, the head of a dog, bat-like wings, horns and a tail. For more than 250 years this mysterious creature is said to prowl through the marshes of Southern New Jersey and emerge periodically to rampage through the towns and cities." It goes on to recount the creature's "popular" origin: "The most widely held belief about the origin of the Jersey Devil is that Mrs. Leeds, a resident of Estellville, was distraught when she learned she was expecting for the thirteenth time. In disgust, she cried out, "Let it be the devil!" The story continues that the child arrived and it was a baby devil. The creature then gave a screech unfolded its wings and flew out the window and into the adjacent swamp."[6]

The more likely truth about this lovely baby lies with the character of the father, Daniel Leeds. Throughout the latter part of the 17th Century and well into the Eighteenth, Daniel Leeds warred with Quakers via a series of scandalous pamphlets, such as *The Innocent Vindicated from the Falsehoods and Slanders of Certain Certificates* (1695). This put Quakerism founder George Fox into a bout of apoplexy, forcing him to respond to Leeds's accusations with *The Case Put and Decided* (1699), which was his argument that

Quakerism was unjustly accused of "any theological wrongdoing."[7] After which he followed up with *Satan's Harbinger Encountered ... Being Something by Way of Answer to Daniel Leeds* (1700), which publically

Illustration depicting the Jersey Devil, from The Philadelphia Post, 1909,

accused Leeds of being in league with the Devil. This is what stood in for a flame war in the olden days. So with Leeds the eternal enemy of Quakers, is it any wonder that his thirteenth fruit of his loins accused of being a literal devil? The "sins of the father" and all that.

Yet the idea of a literal creature from hell gallivanting through New Jersey is not only too tempting to resist, it also explains a lot about New Jersey. Although it wasn't first described in public record until 1909. "It is from

[6] "Jersey Devil and Folklore", Pinelands Preservation Alliance. http://www.pinelandsalliance.org/history/devil/

[7] Regal, Brian. 2013. "The Jersey Devil: The Real Story." The Committee for Skeptical Inquiry. Skeptical Inquirer Volume 37.6, November/December. https://www.csicop.org/si/show/the_jersey_devil_the_real_story

if you ignore all the snarky critics, especially David N. Butterworth who wrote on Rotten Tomatoes, "Anyone who quickly denounced Madonna's *Swept Away* as being the worst film of 2002 clearly hadn't seen *13th Child*." (Careful with that edginess, Dave):

13th Child (or *The 13th Child: Legend of the Jersey Devil*) (2002), which admittedly is as much a take on *The Omen* as it is a take on our regional devil, it has a great cast: Cliff Robertson, Leslie-Anne Down, Robert Guillaume, Peter Jason—even Christopher Atkins. Is it great? No. Is it *Shriek of the Mutilated*? No, it is not. So take that for what it's worth.

The Loch Ness Monster.

Now, for my money, there is no better cryptid than the original Scottish mama herself. While legend has the creature existing for centuries, with reports as far back as the Sixth Century, "Nessie" wasn't made an official monster until 1933, when "water bailiff" and "part-time journalist" Alex Campbell, filed a report to the *Inverness Courier* on a particularly slow news day that a couple saw a "dragon or pre-historic animal" lumbered around the Loch. Since television was still decades away, the *Daily Express* published, on December 6, 1933, the first photograph of the monster, taken by one Hugh Gray, which prompted an order from the Secretary of State for Scotland to local police to prevent anyone attacking the monster. Suddenly, Scotland came down with Nessie Fever.

Over the years, hundreds—if not thousands—of privately-funded expeditions into the Lake (sorry,

these sightings that the popular image of the creature—batlike wings, horse head, claws, and general air of a dragon—became standardized."[8]

If you visit enough of New Jersey, you can discover all sorts of paraphernalia related to the creature—their NHL hockey team is, of course, The New Jersey Devils—and it's had a respectable cinematic representation including:

Carny (2009) also aka *Jersey Devil*, starring Lou Diamond Phillips.

The Barrens (2012), aka *The Jersey Devil*, directed by Darren Lynn Bousman (who we love for *Repo!* and tolerate for *Saw II*.)

But the best one in my opinion,

---

[8] Ibid. Seriously, check this site out for all sorts of wonderous goodies.

Loch) have produced...well, I believe "bupkis" is the official term. But that hasn't stopped the fascination with the possibility that it's still down there, somewhere, an ancient dinosaur pretending to be a log.

The majority of films featuring our favorite Plesiosaur usually utilize her as a MacGuffin. In *What a Whopper* (1961), a vehicle for pop singer Adam Faith and featuring a cameo by the great Spike Milligan, a writer fakes a Nessie siting to promote his book, only to discover most of the other locals are doing the same thing to drum up additional tourism. Then the real Nessie pops up at the end.

Then there's Billy Wilder's wonderfully confounding *The Private Life of Sherlock Holmes* (1970), the monster is actually a submarine constructed by Mycroft Holmes (Christopher Lee) for Her Majesty's Secret Service. (Much like the "creature" in Brian Trenchard-Smith's Henry Thomas-starring *Frog Dreaming* (1986), released in the US as *The Quest* (snore)—in the otherwise

charming movie, the MaGuffin for Thomas' young cryptozoologist turns out to be a steam shovel gone amok).

There have been dozens upon dozens of documentaries on the creature, its lore, its appeal, its turn-ons and dreams, but few, as far as I can tell, films in which the creature is the major antagonist. Sure, there's *The Loch Ness Horror* (1982—see review). Of all the Cryptids, Nessie is generally depicted as gentle, helpful, generous with its time, a kind and thorough lover, and rarely a source of destruction. Which is incredibly distressing, as everyone knows, thanks to Henry Silva in *Amazon Women on the Moon*, that Nessie was, indeed, Jack the Ripper.

Bullshit or not?

Above: Mycroft's Submarine from The Private Life of Sherlock Holmes.
Copyright The Mirisch Corporation.
All Rights Reserved.

Above: Thomas Berdinski (left) as "Sascratch", pictured with "Book Binder of the Dead", Pat Reese.
Photo taken at Cinema Wasteland, the Happiest Place on Earth.
All Photos courtesy Thomas Berdinski

At many conventions throughout the land you will encounter a beast unlike any other. The official mascot of *The Italian Zombie Movie*, the one and only Sascratch. A creature unlike any other...well, we'll let you hear it from him. I was able to grab a few words with his creator Tom Berdinski about film making and the beast known as SASCRATCH!

Exploitation Nation: What got you into the movie making business?

Thomas Berdinski: Nope—I'm not into the movie making "business"! Any time a film making project starts to turn into a business I get away from it. I've made films since I was 8-years-old for the enjoyment of the process. Sure, I take on projects for payment but only if I love the project, enjoy working with the people involved, and only if it fits into my leisure schedule. I have a great day job. I just happen to like to spend my

free time making films. I avoid the business of movie making. Most of my least favorite films are products of the movie "business".

EN: Where does Sascratch come from?

TB: Sascratch will tell you he is the half-human/half-sasquatch result of an involuntary insemination by Bigfoot that took place during any number of 1970's cryptid exploitation films, but the truth is I needed a way to get my micro-budget films noticed. When our first feature, *The Italian Zombie Movie* (*IZM*), came out in 2009, the glut of no-budget, DV-lensed zombie movies was beginning. Rather than moodily sit at my vendor table while autograph seekers passed by, I decided to create "Sascratch: The IZM Mascot" to get people to at least notice that there was something unusual about us...

Sascratch would take crazy photos with patrons and put them all over social media, flirt with every actress in sight, and because he loves horror movies, strike up conversations about every horror movie t-shirt he saw worn. But Sascratch was really just the beginning... We used all sorts of gimmicks and stunts to get people to stop by our tables including a fish bowl full of brightly colored intestines folks could handle, contests and games, slot cars they could race for DVD deals—almost anything—just so we could talk about our films and projects. It worked pretty well for us!

EN: Any plans for him to appear in more movies?

TB: Sascratch made his first movie appearance in a short called *The Giant Rubber Monster Movie* —Aren't my titles creative? In this film, an evil vegetarian travels from the future to wipe out all of the Earth's edible animals using giant monsters. Fortunately, a rebellious stowaway gets control of one of the giant monsters (Sascratch) and uses him to fight back. It was an homage to "Johnny Sokko's Flying Robot" and other 1970's era giant monster TV shows. This short was so popular for us that we decided to expand the story into a feature length film filled with 70's style miniature effects that should release in 2018. In the meantime, Sascratch has appeared on several horror-hosted TV shows, including *Midnite Mausoleum*, which aired the *IZM* double feature. There were several "summer camp" themed skits during that show that were a blast!

EN: Your massive two parter *Italian Zombie Movie* seemed like a massive undertaking. What was something you learned to never do again after making that movie?

TB: Hmm, I think I learned to not be so nice about scheduling... The real

reason *The Italian Zombie Movie* was a two-parter was actor scheduling! We had periods of downtime where an actor or actress was (sometimes suddenly) unavailable, but I had all the zombies made-up so I would quickly write new scenes for the available actors! Weekend shoots like these went on for 2-3 years! I ended up adding a lot of jokes and plot twists that I hadn't intended, but when I looked it all over I decided to release it as a double feature. We even had a two weekend premiere at our local indie theater. The double feature approach cost us some DVD sales initially, but surprisingly (to me) nearly every festival and convention we approached accepted and showed both features! Later, I re-cut and re-released it as a single two-hour film called *IZM – The Grindhouse Cut* for folks with more realistic attention spans. Both versions have fans and I'm very appreciative of that, but no, if I can help it I'll stick strict to schedules and 90 minute films!

EN: What was something you did better because of that movie?

TB: Well, to be completely honest, *IZM* was a "point and shoot" film. In those early days of DV, the affordable cameras had limited capabilities, and my skills as a photographer were not strong. *IZM* is a very "flat" looking film because our equipment and my camera skills weren't enough to give the film that nice depth-of-field you see in films shot with DSLRs today. We were creative with our lighting and camera angles, but when I watch it today I wish we'd had better cameras and more skills. Since then I've become pretty good with DSLRs and interchangeable lenses. You'll

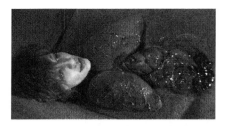

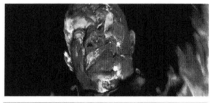

certainly notice the difference in *Giant Rubber Monster Movie 2*.

EN: Sascratch attends many conventions. Tell us the most bizarre Sascratch story from a convention?

TB: Hmm, not knowing who your audience is I'll choose a PG rated adventure: So, at the end of a long day of being Sascratch, I stepped into the hotel elevator, carrying props from our table including the fish bowl full of intestines. A few floors up, a guy and his girlfriend got on the elevator. They quickly told me they were fans of *IZM* and before I could thank them, the guy reached into the fish bowl, pulled out a 18" long intestine and swallowed it. He swallowed it whole. Now, our intestines are made of boiled pig casings, Jell-O, stuffing, bread crumbs and Kool-Aid to color them. They are so sweet they seem to ferment after a few days. This was still a "fresh" intestine but it had been handled by dozens of horror convention patrons at this point. They are NOT meant to be eaten! Expecting him to vomit, I stepped back, but he simply belched and proceeded to kiss his girlfriend on the mouth. She then pulled out her phone, I assumed to call 911, but instead she snapped a selfie with me and I never saw either of them again. That entire night I was awake expecting a call from a Poison Control Unit!

EN: From the multitude of hats you wear when making a movie, which is your favorite hat and why?

TB: When I decided to make *IZM* I really wanted to do everything. I wanted to write it, to raise the money, cast it, appear in it, direct it, shoot it, design the creatures and effects, compose the music, edit it – I wanted to experience every part of making a feature. Now, many years and films later later, I mostly enjoy post production work: Editing, composing music and sounds effects, and creating visual effects. Since *IZM*, I've edited and helped with post production on a number of other filmmaker's shorts and features. There's something very rewarding about assembling a project, polishing it up, or just doing all the little things to make it better. Composing music is probably what I'm best known for since I*ZM*, but special effects have fascinated me since I was a child. And by special effects I really mean miniature effects, monster costumes and make-up effects. I've spent countless hours on the special effects for *GRMM2* and I can't wait to show them off! Special effects are like making magic.

EN: What's the one question you always wished someone would ask and never has?

TB: How much money can I give you for your next feature?" Okay, no one will EVER ask me that question so here's a better question: "Why don't you want to go to Hollywood and make movies?" I like making movies for me. I like the movie making process to be something I do for fun first. If the end result makes some money, that's great and I'll use that money on the next film. I love making movies at my own pace, so I can experiment and rewrite and even re-shoot things. I think being totally independent is the only way I can do things that way. When I take on projects for other people's films I make sure I have the time I need to be able to enjoy it. Film making is what I do for fun and that's how I plan to keep it. (Unless you really going to ask me my first question and you're willing to give me around $25,000,000 ;-)

A big thank you to Tom for answering my questions. And remember, the next time you're at a horror convention and a bizarre half-man, half-, well, something approaches you, never fear. It's Sascratch!

Be sure to visit Sascratch at www. facebook.com/GRMM1/

IT CAME FROM ARKANSAS:

THE LEGEND OF BOGGY CREEK LIVES ON AS A NOT-SO-SPECIAL EDITION DVD
by William J. Wright

This really is a review of the DVD release of *The Legend of Boggy Creek*; I promise. Bear with me, bad movie fans, I will get into this analysis of what has to be the fourth or fifth best use a rented gorilla suit in cinematic

history soon(and, by the way, the best use of a rented gorilla suit *still* goes to 1953's *Robot Monster*). But first, I have to get this off my chest:

DVDs and Blu-ray discs are too expensive. Like the rent, the cost of entertainment on video is just too damned high for the discerning cinephile. Allow me to modify that statement: *Good* entertainment is too expensive. There's no shortage of cinematic flotsam and jetsam out there for cheap from five buck sell-through releases of last summer's dubious blockbusters to obscure and unwatchable Kung Fu theater rejects (Bruce Li?) and the latest in Disney inspired cartoon knock-offs(*Ratatoing? Tangled Up?* Bring these home and your kids are sure to take revenge in their choice of your inevitable extended care facility). As tempting as Mill Creek's latest 500 movie box set of "classic" thrillers may be, you will be disappointed. You will end up with a shelf full of lousy movies with ugly box art for which even the least reputable second-hand dealer won't give you trade credit. You will own multiple copies of *The Giant Gila Monster* and *The Killer Shrews*. You will bring shame upon your house. As of this writing average retail price of a typical disc is still in the neighborhood of $15 to $25 and still a far cry from the cost of a VHS cassette in the early days of the VCR (I remember seeing an ad for the original Thorne/EMI VHS release of *Dawn of the Dead* for $100 back in 1985 and thinking that was just about the price of a man's soul — but if you ordered it from Fantaco, it came with a poster!), the digital entertainment revolution is at last firmly in the grasp of the average movie fan even without taking the internet, streaming video services and good old fashioned piracy into account. However, if your taste in movies is obsessive and leans toward the weird and obscure, you just can't

survive without the latest and greatest in special edition Steelbook discs with multiple cuts and commentary tracks from the cast and crew ranging from the director all the way down to craft services, be prepared to pay. Specialty distributors like Anchor Bay and Dlue Underground, while being the horror and cult aficionado's best friend by regularly re-issuing once rare genre favorites like *The Evil Dead*, can also be deadly enemies of the superfan's wallet. These niche distributors know their customer base beyond intimately and has it pegged as the nation of rabid completists that it is knowing full well that the marks (read "loyal customers") must have every shred of memorabilia and frame of video associated with the films they love. How many extended/collector's/ director's editions of say, *Army of Darkness* can the market bear? Personally, I stopped counting at three and that was over ten years ago, but if so much as any previously unreleased footage of Bruce Campbell's colonoscopy turns up you can bet there will be more.

Nevertheless, when you wade through the muck of the discount bin, you occasionally get lucky. Which brings us back to the strange case of *The Legend of Boggy Creek,* the *Citizen Kane* (or, at least, the *Smokey and the Bandit*) of fake Bigfoot docudramas and a genuine, beloved cult classic that has inexplicably escaped the deluxe treatment by any studio or distributor and tragically continues to occupy that great public domain video ghetto alongside *The Brain that Wouldn't Die* and *Werewolf in a Girl's Dormitory*. Frankly, this weird, charmingly goofball film deserves better than to be endlessly

released as a budget disc.

In the 1970's there was a sudden wave of interest in all things paranormal which resulted in a deluge of movies and TV specials about Big Foot, the occult, ESP, UFOs and the Loch Ness Monster which would more or less crescendo in 1977 with Alan Landsburg Productions'"In Search Of" hosted by Leonard Nimoy. At the forefront of this cultural phenomenon was *The Legend of Boggy Creek*, a grainy exploration into the existence of Arkansas' Fouke County Monster, sort of a poor southern relation of the Pacific Northwest's Sasquatch. Written and directed by ad salesman turned auteur Charles B. Pierce who would strike exploitation gold again with 1976's *The Town that Dreaded Sundown* before moving on to more "legitimate" film work such as co-writing the story for Clint Eastwood's 1983 *Dirty Harry* sequel *Sudden Impact, The Legend of Boggy Creek* was shot entirely in the Arkansas Bottom Lands with a cast and crew of locals—mostly high school students, many of whom were allegedly never paid—re-enacting their real life encounters with the legendary beast who, according to newspaper accounts, had made quite a comeback to the area in recent years.

Boggy Creek is a magnificent bad movie that is long on atmosphere and short on virtually everything else. With a framework couched in the nostalgic, boyhood musings of an unnamed narrator, that we are led to assume is the filmmaker (although the film is not actually narrated by Pierce), *Boggy Creek* has the tone of a skid-row version of *The Waltons* crossbred with a Halloween spook show. Everything about this film bears the mark of schizophrenia. It is at times meandering and boring, resembling a travelog through rural Arkansas tailor-made for insomniacs, yet the verite' camera work of the monster attack scenes is often intense and visceral lending an authenticity that the film just doesn't deserve.

Photo copyright P & L. All Rights Reserved.

Many sequences in *The Legend of Boggy Creek* are eerily effective, particularly the monster's protracted midnight assault on one family's secluded, backwoods home. Unfortunately, for every scene in *Boggy Creek* that works, there are a dozen or more lingering scenes of such compelling subject matter as tree branches swaying in the wind. And I would be remiss not to mention all the heart wrenching and totally out of place folk music which makes up much of the soundtrack and specifically the song "Lonely Cry," a poignant tribute to the creature's solitary existence written by Pierce's *Sudden Impact* writing partner Earl E. Smith and sung by Pierce himself (credited as "Chuck Bryant") over the film's end credits. Here's a sample:

> *Hear the sulfur river flow,*
> *Rising when the storm cloud blows.*
> *And this is where the creature goes,*
> *Safe within a world he knows.*
> *Perhaps he dimly wonders why,*
> *There is no other such as I.*
> *To touch, to love, before I die,*
> *To listen to my lonely cry.*

This would be a touching sentiment were it not for the fact that, among other atrocities, we've witnessed the Fouke Monster frighten a kitten to death.

Like all great bad movies, *The Legend of Boggy Creek* is incredibly self-assured in its complete awfulness. The deadpan narration (provided by Vern Stierman who would also lend his voice to *The Town that Dreaded Sundown*) features some lines that would make Edward D. Wood Jr. blush, my personal favorite being: "He shot part of his foot off in a boating accident" (huh?).

The disc on which I'm basing this review is the out-of-print Sterling Entertainment release, which sports the ponderous title of *Charles B. Pierce's Original The Legend of Boggy Creek, A True Story,* boasts some of the most laughably threadbare bonus features ever committed to DVD. The alleged "production notes" are merely still frames from the opening credits reduced to the size of postage stamps and arranged artlessly on the screen. As for the transfer itself, the film looks as lousy, underexposed and grainy as it ever has, but don't get me wrong, that's part of the film's charm. This material shouldn't look too clean.

To reiterate my initial thesis, I have never seen a film so desperately

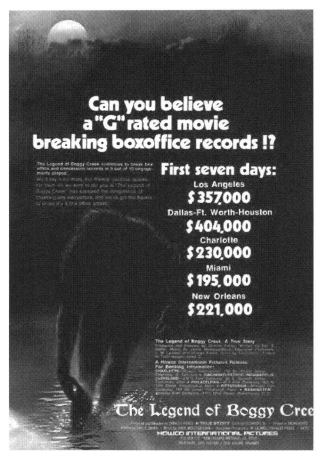

in need of some kind of commentary track (unfortunately, we'll never hear a director's commentary, Charles B. Pierce died in 2010 at the age of 71) or extensive "making of" material.

Although it is now considered a semi-forgotten gem of cult cinema and a prime example of "so-bad-it's-good" filmmaking, it's important to remember *The Legend of Boggy Creek* within the context of its original release to fully understand its importance. Chuck Pierce's $160,000 monster flick grossed $20 million in it's initial U.S. release placing it alongside *The Godfather, Cabaret* and *Deliverance* as one of the top ten box office draws of 1972 — a virtual, if not literal, impossibility for a low-budget, G-rated (yes, *G-rated*) indie in the 21st century. If that doesn't warrant a better, more extensive treatment on home video, nothing does. I am praying that one of the bigger specialty distributors (and I'm looking at you, Lion's Gate/Anchor Bay) will pick up the *Boggy Creek* rights and do this monster justice. Currently, *The Legend of Boggy Creek* can be had for a modest sum (on DVD only, no Blu-ray as of this writing) via mail order from Cheezy Flicks Entertainment, or it can be seen for free on most popular streaming services including several uploads on YouTube of varying, but uniformly poor quality. Naturally, the above is subject to change.

So, is this a negative review? Even I'm not absolutely certain. Somehow, this bad little film works its way into your psyche and takes up permanent residence. This film is utterly awful, and I love every frame of it. It must be seen to be believed. Love it or hate it, *The Legend of Boggy Creek* is, at least, sincere in it's intent and effective in spite of itself.

48

In Search Of (ISO): Bigfoot
THE LOST TRANSLATIONS OF MARK, JOHN, & HENRIQUE...
HE'S THE NEW GUY...
Relatively, if Not Biblically, Speaking...

...By Dr. Rhonda Baughman

Above: The team behind ISO: L-R: Henrique Couto, John Oak Dalton, Mark Polonia. Photo by John Oak Dalton. All images courtesy of Camp Motion Pictures. All Rights Reserved.

Cryptozoology "can come in from the cold" as its Wiki rawrs. And I agree. We've just discovered some kind of new, goddamn spider/scorpion[1] hybrid of nightmarish proportion that it's feasible for me now to believe in "hidden animals". #goteambigfoot

The original subtitle for this article could have been "Endorphins!"— since they began to flow freely (and after a brief hiatus that I can only blame on my move to the high altitude of Colorado Springs). At any rate,

these welcome chemicals returned after my interview with filmmaker Mark Polonia[2], when I realized how

[1] My apocalypse has this thing in it: http://www.dailymail.co.uk/sciencetech/article-4758014/Terrifying-image-shows-spider-scorpion-HYBRID-Arizona.html.

[2] Understand, I ran a little shop called the Movie Exchange from 2001-2003 and the VHS box and goofy cover art of Mark Polonia's *Blood Red Planet* sat quietly on a shelf and stared at me all day, every day, until one gray Canton moment, it mysteriously vanished. Probably into one of my hoodlum friend's backpacks. But really, who knows? You might know him from the early relationship he had with Camp Motion pictures and as the writer/director/editor/star of *Splatter Farm* (1987) (from that lovable genre of '80s 'shot on video in someone's backyard with sketchy film stock boon' that is often derided by filmmakers of a higher caliber who take themselves way too seriously or that group of assholes/douche critics who have never made a film but know they could if only (insert myriad

49

much fun I had—how much insight I was given! So, thank goodness for Polonia —he may have saved my life without even knowing it (lack of endorphins can lead to crying which can lead to depression which can lead to … well, you *know*).

But then again, I hear that quite a bit—that is, Mark (and his brother and collaborator John Polonia) have helped many people in the biz, by offering a helping hand, a leg up, some shoulders to cry on, and quite possibly other body parts we didn't have time to discuss. In other words—the Polonia boys have been in the industry for a long time and are good guys to work with—smart guys, artistic guys— the ones you want on your team when it gets down to the nitty gritty. *ISO* screenplay writer John Oak Dalton[3] and cinematographer Henrique Couto[4] backed up this statement when I interviewed them as well.

Mark Polonia's friend, producer, and collaborator Mike (Raso) "recently purchased some found Super 8 Bigfoot footage which in turn

Above: Dalton and Couto. Photo by Dalton. Below: Dawson Hilfiger, Nicholas Olson (center). Sophie Guss and Grace Hines (crouching). Photo by Anthony Polonia.

became the catalyst for *ISO* which had been in our minds for a long time," according to Mark. "We'd just finished shooting *Land Shark* in LA[5]

---

excuses here). Right.

[3] Lovely man who generously devoted his time to be a guest speaker at a college I helped oversee in Indianapolis in 2016—and who, as I told my student body—has written numerous films I know they've seen and if they remain nowhere else than the fevered dreams of video store shelves of our youth, and/or local Wal-Mart bins, then no offense, but that's more than most writers ever get—so understand, children you are in the presence of artistic greatness! I did get a few nods of understanding and one kid who asked if this info would be on a quiz. That college is now closed. May it RIP.

[4] I met Couto when he was just a youngster who wore silly fun pants on the set of *Demon Divas in the Lanes of Damnation*. Couto still wears those silly pants and is still quite young, but he's no longer a kid. He's a force to be reckoned with on the indie movie scene—and he'll kill you …

with kindness. Or a drive-by Dick pic.

[5] Not to be confused with the recent *Dick Shark* from director Bill Zebub who cast Erin Brown, who also worked with Raso under her Misty Mundae moniker who … ah, fuck it. The shark and cryptozoology sync runs deep and long— best not to jump in just yet. Besides, a nickname for me at work is Megalodon Nom Nom, so fuck you. While we giggle at Dick/Land/House Shark, know that the Sharknado series has generated some folks A LOT of dough. My very own Sugar Shark can be seen via my FB page, as it is the basis for a comic, not yet a film. Call me if you wanna buy it though. Thanks.

50

*L-R: Sophie Guss, Nicholas Olson, Dawson Hilfiger, Grace Hines.
Photo by Anthony Polonia.*

and *ISO* was the next step. It's is a kid-friendly teem film about a son looking for his missing father. In the interim, they meet up with a juvenile bigfoot who was separated from its parents, so it all turns into a quest. I have worked for Camp Motion pictures for years so the whole project really just fell into place. The parameters were that we were going to shoot on 4K, it had to be kid-friendly and PG, and there must be kids in the cast. It was also inevitable I would work with John and Henrique," he says. "And I like to work with people, to collaborate. It's how I run a set. Sure, the director has the final say or things don't get done, but you don't get much out of people if you bark orders at them."

"*ISO* was a little more complicated logistically than I am used to, but I had a great team with me," Mark continues. "We had a few weather issues, and in productions with kids, things can go south pretty fast, but it didn't on this shoot—everything went pretty smoothly for the duration of the shoot [six days]. And everyone had something to bring to the table," he

says. As a side note, Polonia tells me that *ISO* harkens back to the days of SUNN classics[6].

Mark worked daily, from 630am to midnight, non-stop—and had his hands in many aspects of the film's creation. He says, "…We shot on 4K. And I don't work like some do on the big Hollywood productions, where the director arrives on set, looks into the camera for a bit, and that's it. After early morning set-up, we'd work with the kids, since they can only so many hours. After that, until midnight, we did the scenes with the adults. We broke things down as best we could while taking people's time into account,"[7] he says. "Then we'd get up and do it again the next day."

"On some level," Polonia continues, "you're really dealing with artists. As long as the vision is kept, it's okay to let others have input, let others win. People really do need to feel like what they have to say matters. That their input matters. Because ultimately, it does. A director's attitude matters, too. I've been on sets where people did bark orders, no one was allowed to give input—and those are not fun sets. Keeping people engaged and happy, giving them a say—it goes a long way. On my own low-budget sets, not having a good time has never been an issue for me. I do follow the Golden Rule[8] and movie sets can be

6 https://en.wikipedia.org/wiki/Sunn_Classic_Pictures

7 Oh yeah? Maybe corporate America should take that into account as well. #myworkisnotyetdone #corporatehorror

8 If you don't actually know what this is, well, here … come a little closer to me. Smell this raggy. Does it … does it smell like chloroform to you?

stressful, so I like to have fun and so when working together, there's really no limit to what can be accomplished," Mark says.

"By all accounts," he says, "*ISO* was a really big production: bullies and bad guys with guns for a shootout, good guys, two Bigfoots, and a car chase. We were loaned a '67 Dodge Charger for this film—we didn't pay a dime for it, and so I try to be respectful of people's things, too. The gentleman who loaned it to us—he didn't have to do that, but he wanted to. People really opened their doors for us on *ISO* and we have some really nice added elements because of it," Mark says.

Additionally, he tells me, *ISO* is shot without the element of cell phones —that is, no video recording of encounters, no quick way to take photos. "We wanted to focus on the story," he says, "and not be bogged down by the technology. Without the gore, too, I can tell this will really be a different film from me than people are used to." And while editing begins soon, "the footage looks great so far" he says. And frankly, I like the idea of the innocence of life before cell phones, before their endless gadgets were available for tinkering, long lines, and 'this shit is on fire on an airplane' lawsuits.

We come to meat of the interview. I want to know if Mark is a believer. A *true* Bigfoot believer.

"My philosophy is simple. There are things, plenty of things, in this world that we can't explain," Mark says. I quietly think *a Trump presidency* to myself, but do not say it, because I know what he means, really. And I agree wholeheartedly. "Sure

Photo by John Oak Dalton.

there's a small percentage who are complete crackpots, but there are also too many people who have nothing to gain, only their credibility to lose, by admitting they've seen ghosts, UFOs, aliens, life after death, for example. Teachers, judges, real everyday people who don't know each other but can describe the same phenomena," he says.

All of my ghost stories run through my head—and I have a few. And that's when my endorphins really kick in. I realize Mark Polonia is people. *MY people.*

"Do you want to hear a ghost story?" he asks.

"Yes," I say, trying to play cool, casual, as if I'm not so excited I might squee.

And so he tells me.

"So you see," he says, after the story, "it's not scary, but I just can't explain it."

He also tells me he later met a man who could corroborate the same ghost story—a man who had seen the same thing, that Mark had never met prior to his ghostly encounter.

Oh, I'm not going to tell you the ghost story—it wouldn't be the same if I did. You really need to hear Mark tell it.

"There's so much out there that people cannot easily put the information into boxes as they're used to. I know how hard it is for some people to believe. But personally, even if I can't fully believe, I don't disbelieve either. There's too much that defies description, explanation, easy categorization—history tells us that," he says.[9]

Bigfoot vs. Zombies, Polonia's 2016 mad scientist release, isn't as goofy as it sounds. I mean, yes, it's goofy, but the plot concerns a body farm[10] as opposed to solo cryptozoology—which is relevant, current events—not just history. Polonia knows his budget, knows he's not reaching for the Academy Award this year but does try to tell a good story. And like those SUNN classics of yore, Polonia and fans of the SUNN Classics have learned something. "It was never derogatory. No one ever poked fun. SUNN presented the facts. And they did it well and for a long time," Mark says.

Polonia remains in love with dinosaurs and has been since he was four years old. Some cryptozoo lovers think dinosaurs may still exist in some exotic, scarcely reachable part of the globe. Although he admits *Saurians* (1994) was cheap, it was his attempt at an adventure-type movie. Frankly, cheap and awkward or not, this film still holds a special place in the hearts of those who, like me, love puppets and stop motion and are horrifically bored with CGI.

Jurassic Prey (2015), proof Mark has not given up on the dinosaur flick, was originally titled *Meat Eaters*. A confused critic asked why the plural when there was only one dinosaur. Mark explains, "The real predator in the film was the female." As an English/Lit major I can empathize with Mark there—symbolism often zips right over many heads. But he considers it his more successful dinosaur flick. Polonia's IMDB profile is long and distinguished, if not immediately recognizable by the masses then certainly by industry fans and the occasional symbolism supporter.

Polonia is happy with this career. He's not done, but he is happy. He has no regrets about putting all his eggs in one basket. He followed a plan. He didn't just have dreams, he had goals. He and his brother have worked together for a long time. They were 17 years old when starting out, and only 18 when *Splatter Farm* (1987) hit the scene and gave them instant cult and celebrity status. Let me write it again: they weren't just dreamers; they set goals. Made it all happen. And again, Mark has no illusions about where his place is. "In my arena, success really is a state of mind," he says.

"There's no magic formula and if

---

[9] I know what he means. It's how I felt when I learned the word 'hygge'. There's no easy English/American translation for it, but as a concept, once I understood it, I nearly screamed aloud: "OMG. THERE'S A WORD FOR THAT! I KNEW IT! I JUST DIDN'T *KNOW* IT!

[10] There were six in the US. Now there are seven: https://www.forbes.com/sites/kristinakillgrove/2017/02/28/new-body-farm-opens-in-florida-becomes-7th-in-us/#d29815628645

I was in this to make money, I would have chosen to sell drugs instead. I certainly would have made more money. But I have a passion. Making movies is what I want to do. What I have to do. It's a process and I come from an artistic, if not autistic, family as well. I like taking ideas and shaping them from paper to screen. To do this, day after day, for 30 years, still fascinates me. I still see the magic in it. As an adult, the magic often gets beaten out of you. So I never let go of the wonderment that I had as a kid," he says.

Although he's hit many of the goals: VHS distribution, DVD distribution, foreign distribution, cable TV— he would still like to see a film on the big screen. "I want to keep trying, look forward … I like to stop and remember but not for too long. My idea is always to try until I'm satisfied. I want my tombstone to say: He died trying," Mark says, not laughing, but probably smiling.

ISO cinematographer Henrique Couto and screenplay writer John Oak Dalton still have that sense of child-like magic and wonderment that Polonia talks about—and no one is quite ready for the tombstone. Case in point, John tells me: "I've done seven movies for Mark and four for Henrique and I was pretty confident they would get along—both are huge horror fans, have had great success and longevity in the industry, and are collaborative on set. They pulled up to my hotel in Wellsboro with Mark's son Anthony

L-R: Titus Himmelberger, Natalie Hallead, Nicholas Olson, Sophie Guss, Jeff Kirkendall, "who worked on the crew only for this one," sez Dalton. Photo by Paige K. Davis.

and I kind of looked in the windshield and thought, *I can't believe I'm seeing this*," he says.

Rhonda: "So, is this all for the fun of it? The fame and glory of B-movie stardom … or … are you a true Bigfoot believer?"

John: "I'm not ruling anything out. My son-in-law is a strong Bigfoot believer. (And just look at the stuff that comes out of the deep ocean, or somebody finds in a jungle somewhere. I think I could do any of those, except maybe a Mothman story. That scares me too badly.) When I was doing research for the first Bigfoor movie I wrote—*Among Us*—I became more of a believer in cryptozoology. Funny thing was, I put a lot of real-life cases in the screenplay and the director (in this case *also* Mark Polonia) thought I was making everything up."

Rhonda: "There's a true testament to your writing ability. Why did you want to become involved in this production, specifically?"

John: "I got involved in this movie because A.) I want to be the first screenwriter with two Bigfoot movies on my resume and B.) I enjoy working with Mark Polonia. [Bonus C.] When I found out Henrique Couto was involved I legit started thinking about all the great dream team films—first off—*The Good, The Bad, and The Ugly.* To add one more, Brett Piper[11] was there on the last day helping me out."

If you've ever worked with John and Mark, in any capacity, then you know what it means to work with industry badasses. So, when working with someone like Henrique, it's much the same—and you also know what a good time you're going to have—working with someone so genuine, so funny, so giving, and so smart that … Wait. Did that guy just send me a Dick pic while I'm writing this interview up? Like a Dick Van Dyke Dick pic? A random, drive-by, FB Dick pic? He most certainly did. Just knowing filmmakers like HC are out there—I feel a little bit more hopeful about the world in general. Dick pic or no.

Henrique: "Mark is highly motivated and confident director. I was contacted by the production to come in and help them make the slickest best film we could and in 4K. I was pretty excited. I do cinematography a lot here and there but usually only on my own feature productions. I always like a new adventure."

John: "I didn't get my first break from Mark, but Mark directed the first screenplay I wrote that turned into an actual movie—also a Bigfoot movie, a long while ago. If you talk to him long

enough you find out he has given a lot of other b-movie people a leg up at one time or another early on in their careers (Some day, ask him how he traded Don Adams a burning house for a stripper). He is very conscientious and collaborative and incredibly prolific—not only making movies but getting them distributed and seen everywhere. I was very eager to see the Mark and Henrique collaboration because I think they are a lot alike—similar set demeanor and set atmosphere, hard workers interested in tech and the industry; they love movies, have gathered cult followings as well as each having a loyal, talented troupe of actors and crew people they use from movie to movie."

While there's no specific release date for ISO, it's all good. Look for it in the next year. In the interim, you have a little bit of time to locate and watch the back catalogs of our mosr recent three wise men: Mark Polonia, John Oak Dalton, and Henrique Couto. I bet they even have some incense lying around if you really needed it.

---

[11] On Brett Piper: You can find him on IMDB. com but all I needed to know is that he prefers old school special FX over CGI. #mypeople #score

GINGERSQUATCH!

Making the Myth

By Doug Waltz

The movie started like many bad ideas, amongst friends on a drive to the convention known as Cinema Wasteland. At this time I was unaware of the actual term 'Gingersquatch' and thought we were being clever. The concept of the film was worked out before we made it home from the convention that weekend. My two partners in crime, Christopher Young and Michael Gillespie said they would help get it done.

Two weeks later there was a script.

Nothing would be the same.

I did have a little experience with some short subject backyard films. In addition to that there is a competition ever year at the local cable access company where teams of people shoot a short film over a weekend. Throw in eight years of producing my own horror host program, The Basement of

Baron Morbid and what could go wrong?

The basic premise is that a small, red headed boy is left in the woods and raised by Sasquatch. Years later he is captured by the government and studied. When they discover that all he likes to do is drink beer, watch TV and eat salty snacks, they decide he is no threat to anyone and release him into the modern world to fend for himself.

But, there is a secret organization, headed by a madman bent on revenge for the death of his brother at the hands of a much younger *Gingersquatch*.

A mishap with beef jerky sends the beast on a rampage and he meets a girl, they have a baby (The gestation period for Gingersquatch is very short) and are on the run from the military.

See, a great script right? Later I discovered that while it does manage to get from point A to point B, it was pretty short. More on that later.

So, we started shooting. Mostly weekends as I had started a new job at a call center. My youngest son was the baby Gingersquatch and my oldest was the adult version. Luckily, they both have red hair so little special effects were needed. We did give my oldest son, Seann, some extra hair coming out of his shirt and some huge mutton chops. My youngest, Daniel, we just rolled in the dirt to make him look scruffy.

I am fortunate that a lot of my friends are musicians and just let me use whatever music of theirs that I wanted. I decided on Henrique Couto's heartwarming tune, Fuck Everybody, for the montage rampage when the adult Gingersquatch goes off the rails. We grabbed Seann, my two producers and headed downtown. The producers did a live tune of an original tune written by Michael called Shoot 'Em In The Head. Something he wrote for an aborted zombie movie I wrote years before. Then Seann rampages throughout downtown Kalamazoo. He just growled and waved his arms a lot. He ran out of a coffee shop, up and down the stairs of city hall in a Rocky like fashion and then we got one of the best shots in the movie.

There was a wedding shoot going on in front of the Civic Theater. I wanted Gingersquatch to run in front of it making noise. I thought it was a great idea. My producers thought I shouldn't bother them. I ignored their advice and approached the wedding party. Luckily, and unbeknownst to me the bride had read something about the movie in the paper. I had no idea anyone knew we were making a movie. We had shot a few scenes downtown and at the local radio station so, I figured my friend, Rick Shields, one of the news jockeys had probably said something about it on his show and then it got in the local paper.

Anyway, she said yes. We shot it twice and it ended up in the movie. I mocked my producers for being wimps and we continued with the movie.

Between the opening titles of the film that was old, supposedly real, Bigfoot sightings with a tune by The Evil Deaureaux, the song by Michael and the montage tune by Henrique the movie was becoming more of a music concept video than anything else. I even used a song by Mark Baranowski for the love scene that was a throwback to old days of trains going through tunnels, waves crashing on the beach, rockets shooting into the sky and candles melting in time lapse. It was silly, but funny.

When it came time for Gingersquatch to fight ninjas we did an old bit where it was one guy watching the fight and there was punching noises and he reacted to the noises. Christopher did a good job with that. This was better than when he had to deliver lines. If you watch the film pay close attention to when he talks. His accent changes for no apparent reason throughout the film. I didn't catch it during filming as I was shooting the film as well as directing and there was no way I was going to go back and fix it. We left it and it gives the movie a quirk that seems to work.

We were getting close to the end of shooting and had two big scenes left to do. One was Gingersquatch finally dealing with the threat of his nemesis,

Marcus, by crushing his head. Did I mention that my friend Christopher is also a special effects artist? Yeah, that is something he is really good at so he made a really nice looking head that had blood and cable in it. My lovely wife, Martha was in charge of one of the cables that broke during the effect. I told Seann to just keep crushing and wiggling it and we could take care of it in post. I ended up using a series of dissolves that made it look pretty good.

The final scene is where the townspeople chase Gingersquatch through downtown Kalamazoo. I picked a spot near the museum that loops through a huge courtyard. The plan was to chase him, he hides behind a newspaper and gets away.

So, I put out the call for extras on the radio and social media and we ended up with a pretty good sized group.

Now in hindsight, I would have had them start and stop several times to get the shot I wanted. Yeah, that seems like a good idea at the time. I also wrote a scene on the spot with a news reporter and the newspaper was there covering the shoot and taking pictures.

So, yeah instead I had them marathon run the loop…twice. Some of them didn't make it. The fell by the wayside and leaned against buildings. This actually made the shots from the chase scene funnier so, I'm glad I did it. We used Yakety Sax by Boots Randolph and, to date, haven't gotten a cease and desist so, that's good.

That was almost the end of shooting. We had a final scene that ends the movie where Gingersquatch, his new girlfriend and their love child head for the woods where they encounter a Sasquatch named Dave.

In Kalamazoo we have a costume rental shop called The Timid Rabbit. Tony Gerard makes many of the costumes himself and he had a homemade Bigfoot costume. He let us borrow it for free for a credit in the film and I decided to wear it. The thing was hot and unbearable, but we managed to get the shot and it looks

Christopher Young and Seann Walker in Gingersquatch. Photo courtesy of Douglas Waltz.

good.

Now, the film was done, shot and I went into the editing process. I had already edited it in my head so, that wasn't awful.

But, then I had a final cut of about 40 minutes.

That wasn't going to work.

I needed something to make it longer.

Then I got it.

First I needed to get Tabby back in her costume and look very pregnant. Then we had her sitting in a chair and flipping through channels and reacting to what she's watching and then she goes into labor.

Back at the computer I inserted the previously mentioned short films I had made previously as shows on the television. I used the entire short film minus the credits and it put me at a running time of an hour.

My buddy, Stew Miller did artwork for the cover. Chris Seaver agreed to release it on his label and then it was time for the local premiere.

My friend, Matt Dorbin, was in charge of booking shows at the local Blues club, The 411. He got a band to open for us and we showed the movie.

I hid in the back while the place filled up and they showed the film. It felt like torture and the movie felt too damned long to me.

In the end we made enough money to pay for the two clown wigs we needed for the shoot. I gave the rest of the money to the band that opened and we broke even.

To date, I'm pretty sure we haven't made any money from the film. I gave away a lot of copies. I also rereleased it as a director's cut where I whittled it down to 45 minutes. It plays much better that way. It also managed to be an episode of my horror host show. We used the shorter version there. No reason to scare off my three loyal viewers.

Gingersquatch was a fun way to spend time with my friends and make something silly. We accomplished that. We had a good time and there are a few shots that I'm pretty proud of.

What more can you ask for?

For more information on Gingersquatch, hit Doug up on Facebook: facebook.com/douglas. waltz

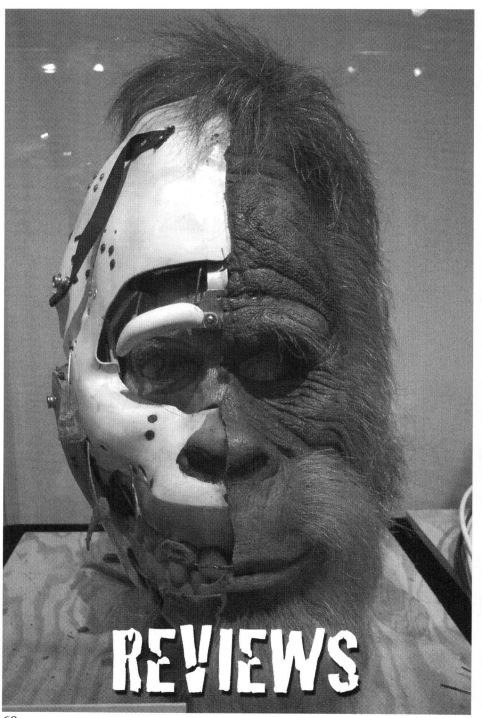

REVIEWS

This issue by: Bill Adcock, Mike Haushalter, Mike Watt.

Abominable (2006)

A paraplegic man who lost his wife and the use of his legs after a fall from "Suicide Rock" (a name that struck no fear into the climbers' hearts, apparently), returns to his mountain home to discover Bigfoot stalking a bridal party at the cabin next door. It's the cryptid equivalent of *Rear Window*.

Ryan Schifrin's debut film is perfectly fine. You don't seek out a Bigfoot film in the hopes of uncovering nuances of the human spirit, after all. You want to see a skunk ape chew people up. And *Abominable* does that well.

Plus, Schifrin packs the film with incredibly fun cameos—Jeffrey Combs as an appropriately weird, oxygen-bound, chainsmoking store clerk; Lance Henriksen as a hunter "who enjoys killing things" other than bigfoot; Dee Wallace and TV's Rex Linn as a hapless farm couple; Matt McCoy, the once and future "affordable Gutenberg", doing his stalwart best as the wheelchair bound hero; our friend and yours Tiffany Shepis as the smartest member of the bridal party (the one who wants to go for help, but has to take a shower instead—geez, Schifrin, make the Troma chick get naked, *whydonthcha*?). Plus: Paul Gleeson as the local sheriff. Everyone gets a nice moment to shine and nobody feels wasted.

And above all, the fun, jazzy score courtesy of his old man, the great Lalo Schifrin, whose scores have graced everything from *Enter the Dragon* to *Cool Hand Luke*. In fact, here the music is spirited—one might even say encouraging and supportive.

Now, the key to any successful Bigfoot movie is the fuzzy guy himself. Designed by Christien Tinsley of Tinsley Transfers, the ol' skunk ape in this case is menacing, yes, in a strange all-over perm, but the face, sharp teeth and all, makes it look like an enraged Merlin Olsen.

Schifrin the younger went on to write and direct a series of shorts, including a segment of the well-made anthology, *Tales of Halloween.*

Tell me that's not Merlin Olsen. Photo copyright Red Circle Productions. All Rights Reserved.

61

Bigfoot, and Merlin Olsen (don't believe that obituary!), continue to be at large. (MW)

The Abominable Snowman (1957). Man, pity the Yeti. One minute you're the top of the cryptozoological world, the next everyone's abandoned you to chase after a bigger, worse-smelling American imitation. Even saddled with as ridiculous name as "Abominable Snowman" via newspapers' bungled mistranslation of the creature's Nepalese name, the Yeti had a considerable moment in the sun throughout the 1950s, spurred by mountaineer Eric Shipton's photographs of alleged Yeti tracks. It was even the target of several high-profile expeditions – supported by the US government, no less, as the expeditions provided a convenient smokescreen for the CIA to keep tabs on those goddamned Russians and the Red Chinese.

It's unsurprising then, that the Yeti swiftly made the jump into popular culture, being a focus of several films in the late 1950s and early 1960s (the

Bumble in 1964's Rankin-Bass special *Rudolph the Red-Nosed Reindeer* being perhaps the most prominent). Of these, my money is on Hammer's 1957 film *The Abominable Snowman* (originally a made-for-TV film, then remade for theatrical release) as the best of the bunch. Directed by Val Guest from a screenplay by Nigel Kneale and starring Peter Cushing (in his second role with the studio that would make his name synonymous with horror) and Forrest Tucker, this film is a study in atmospherics and suspense, making the most of a tiny cast and mostly-enclosed sets.

Cushing stars as Rollason, a British botanist staying as guest of the Lama at the monastery of Rong-Buk high in the Himalayas. Over the objections of his wife, assistant and the Lama himself, Rollason takes an interest in a second expedition that wanders in from the cold – that of Dr. Tom Friend (Tucker), an American in search of the legendary Yeti. Rollason joins Friend's expedition out of curiosity, having heard the legends and wondering if there could be some element of truth to them, while Friend is out solely for the glory of being the first one to bag a Yeti. Tension grows as the two men feud over how best

More like "The Adorable Snowman". Photo copyright Hammer Films. All Rights Reserved.

to find the creature, while Friend's careless glory-seeking gets one assistant killed and imperils the whole expedition. Confrontations with a less-than-friendly Yeti compound the expedition's problems.

I tend to be of the opinion that Nigel Kneale, as a screenwriter, could do no wrong. I've yet to see anything come from his pen that wasn't exceptional, especially when it came to blurring the lines between science fiction and horror. The clash of personalities between Rollason's British stiff-upper-lip and Friend's American brashness is handled well, and the film makes the most of its limited cast to play up the isolation of the setting, making it as much a source of horror as the titular ape-creature. In the field of cryptozoology movies, I would call this one a rare must-see. (BA)

Baby: Secret of the Lost Legend (1985). It's something of a surprise to me, given their prevalence in the cryptozoological literature, that we don't see more movies about relic dinosaurs, the Loch Ness Monster aside. Dinosaurs surviving into the present day are certainly a trope in pulpy adventure movies, but are quite a bit rarer in crypto-cinema. To the best of my knowledge, the 1985 film *Baby: Secret of the Lost Legend*, from Disney's Touchstone imprint, is the only film based on legends of the Mokele-Mbembe, allegedly a man-eating Brontosaurus hiding in the Congo River basin.

Paleontologist Susan Matthews-Loomis (Sean Young) and her husband George (William Katt) are in central Africa, searching for evidence of surviving dinosaurs as the source of the Mokele-Mbembe legend, over the objection of her superior, Dr. Kiviat (Patrick McGoohan).

They soon find their relic Brontosaurs, a small family consisting of two adults and a baby. Unfortunately, they also quickly learn that Kiviat was using Susan to find the Brontosaurs without having to risk his own academic career on following a "crazy theory." Worse, he's brought the army of a local warlord with him to ensure that "his" discovery of living dinosaurs makes it out of Africa. With one of the adult Brontosaurs killed in a hail of gunfire and the other loaded into a cage, Susan and George flee into the jungle with the baby, embarking on a daring plan to free the mother and get both lumbering reptiles to safety deeper in the jungle.

Bearing the Disney touch, *Baby: Secret of the Lost Legend* is a solid enough film; maybe not one worth revisiting again and again, but well worth an initial watch in my estimation. The performances are fairly good throughout, with McGoohan standing out in a rare villainous performance. Likewise, the animatronics used to bring the dinosaurs to life are excellent for the time. They resemble depictions

63

of Brontosaurus from the 1940s, rather than contemporary understanding of how these animals moved and lived; given how descriptions of Mokele-Mbembe resemble this outdated, tail-dragging depiction rather than what we now understand these creatures to have been like, this is actually wholly apropos. (BA)

The Beast And The Vixens (1974)

Sexy college girls Ann (Jacqueline Giroux) and Mary (Uschi Digard) head out to the woods to research some local legends. Along the way they encounter some free loving hippies, an old hunchbacked coot, ruthless crooks, and Sasquatch.

The Beast and The Vixens (aka *The Beauties and the Beast* or—my favorite title--*Desperately Seeking Yeti*) is a low rent Harry Novack/Al Adamson looking softcore roughie with bigfoot and big breasts (courtesy of Uschi Digard). It's uneven mix of sexual encounters, criminals, random hikers and cryptozoology that feels very much like two or more unfinished films stitched together to form a full length feature, topped off with a mondo two minute intro featuring an on screen tree hugging narrator (Lucky Brown, the voice from the opening of Hollywood Chainsaw Hookers) that hard sells the legend of bigfoot and the events that are about to unfold as being true.

In this film Bigfoot is mostly a voyeuristic, women stealing subplot who shows up as needed to keep things interesting and give the film a hook to lure in the punters. For what it's worth the big guy at least seems pretty tall and he looks more Sasquatch-like in costume than ape suit. He even gets a little groping action with one of the sexy extras in in the longer, harder cut of the film included on the DVD. The rest of the film deals with a pair of townie student chicks who hook up with some hippies that some criminals think have stolen their hidden loot. Mostly all of this is just an excuse to get as much bare skin on the screen as possible and exploit the (at the time) superstardom of Bigfoot. Beyond that it offers up some odd humor such as a nude quick draw dream sequence and some running gags involving a rubber duck.

The Beast And The Vixens has been released on DVD a number of times over the years but Retromedia's release is your best bet if you're really looking to add this to your collection. The disc features two cuts of the film both the original 71 minute widescreen theatrical cut and a harder 84 minute uncut print that apparently runs a few minutes longer than any cut ever before offered. It also features a brief commentary track form Fred Olen Ray that offers up a little choice trivia about the film and its cast and as a special bonus the Uschi Digard feature Hollywood Babylon (1972). (MH)

Bigfoot (1970)

Tagline: "Breeds with anything!"

High up in the wilds of the rugged northwest, Sasquatch are kidnapping women to breed and replenish their race. Rick (Christopher Mitchum) knows this all too well after a Bigfoot snatches his gal (Joi Lansing) and smacks him around. When Rick finds out that the local police will not help out he sets off into the night with two greedy hunters, Jasper B. Hawks (John Carradine) and Elmer Briggs (Cristopher's uncle John Mitchum) out to cash in on the Bigfoot legend. Will he be able to save his lady from a fate worse than death?

Competent drive in hokum from producer Anthony Cardoza (*The Beast of Yucca Flats, The Sky Divers, and Night of the Ghouls*), directed by Robert F. Slatzer from a screenplay co-written with James Gordon White (*The Incredible 2-Headed Transplant* and *The Thing with Two Heads*) that cashes in on the Bigfoot craze and biker flicks. It is stuffed to the gills with B-grade actors and has beens including cowboy legend Ken Maynard, James Craig John, Christopher Mitchum, Haji, horror legend John Carradine and the gorgeous Joi Lansing. Roger Ebert puts it best in his own review of the film: "The cast alone convinced me. Let me put it as simply as I can: If you have ever wanted to see a movie starring John Carradine, Joi Lansing, Lindsay Crosby, Chris Mitchum, and Ken Maynard, then '*Bigfoot*' is almost certainly going to be your only chance. Not since Joan Crawford starred in '*Trog!*' has there been such an opportunity." of which I heartily agree.

I first tasted this thick slice of cheese at a 16mm screening at Cinema Wasteland and have been a fan ever since. Its an earnest bit of monster run amuck it the woods that is fun for all, kind of like a small scale redneck King Kong. Sure it's got some rough edges and a lot of scenes of people walking in the woods or pretending to walk in the woods on sound stages and there is some shitty day for night photography but it has so much star power it all seems kind of worthwhile.

Highlights include some very fine speechifying from John Carradine, a bigfoot vs bear smack down, and the dramatic suspense of whether or not Joi's magnificent mammaries will fall out of her top or not (and you're not getting any spoilers from me).

As an added bonus, the exterior shots were filmed in the mountains where several individuals had reported seeing "Bigfoot." (At least according to a footnote at the end of the film's credits.) Some of these locations include Big Bear Lake, the very spot where *The Beast And The Vixens* was filmed. (MH)

Bigfoot Wars (2014)

The town of Boggy Creek (I wonder if it's the same Boggy Creek as the "famous" film) has a problem a big problem Sasquatch! Things are

C. Thomas Howell and E.N. favorite Holt Boggs in Bigfoot Wars. Photo copyright Edgen Films. All Rights Reserved.

not going well for Sheriff Jim Taylor (friend to *E.N.* Holt Boggs) he has anger management issues, a checkered past, politicians breathing down his neck, a hillbilly mafia gang war and to top it all off it is a feral band of sasquatch who are harvesting the locals for food and breeding stock and The sheriff's daughter is their latest victim

A lot of reviewers out there are throwing shade at this one, dwelling on its continuity errors, poor editing, crazy film noir narration and other problems. But in my eyes this is top of the heap B-movie fun at its best, It's the film I want to see every time I watch a Syfy Channel movie of the week; an exciting short and sweet (75 minutes) gore-filled sasquatch clan on the rampage that's light on thinking and all about the action. Not sure if the film seems a bit better than the rest of its ilk because it was based off the book series of the same name from Eric S. Brown, the many fast moving man-in-monster suit bigfoots (pretty imposing ones at that), or the cast of slumming stars (C. Thomas Howell, Billy Blair, and Judd Nelson as a drug addicted comedy relief doctor).

What I do know is it has a ton of blood, guts, and dismemberment, ample T&A, and tons of on-screen sasquatch. All in all it was a fun bigfoot flick and really, what more can you ask for? (MH)

Harry and the Hendersons (1987). Exploitation? Why yes, sir. Exploitation at its finest: '80s Emotional Exploitation!

It is my understanding that this family-friendly, Spielberg-adjacent bit of cryptid comedy, rather than any of the *Boggy Creek* entries that reignited the spark and zeal for the cryptosociety and the Fortean Times in which we live. I'm also given to understand that this movie has torn the crypto-zoological community in two, with people firmly in both pro- and anti-"Harry" camps. For some reason, I find this fascinating. Give any group of a people one subject and they'll figure out how to divide themselves. Usually fairly evenly. Particularly when the stakes aren't that particularly high. Anyway, that's human nature and, really, that's what *Harry and the Hendersons* is all about.

Directed by Spielberg enthusiast and former Michael Nesmith co-

66

conspirator William Dear (*Timerider*), The Hendersons are a nice white nuclear family from the '80s, first seen holding aloft their nine-year-old son's first hunting kill, played in this film by a dead rabbit. We learn that while patriarch George (John Lithgow) loves camping, and the family (Melinda Dillon and two '80s castoffs as the over-cute and swearing / moody eye-rolling kids) loves George so they too profess to love camping, he possesses the soul of an artist, unappreciated by his hunting store-owning father (M. Emmett Walsh). Digesting their meal of murdered rabbit, they depart back to their suburban Seattle climes, ignoring all the nature around them— bear cubs, bobcats, squirrels, swarms of locust—until they ignore one thing too many and manage to run down a sasquatch. Doing what any rational family would do in a sitcom situation, they strap the 400 lb., presumably dead carcass of the mythical creature to their roof and take it home. There is a vague rationale to this, mumbled in haste by Lithgow, but basically it boils down to, "we need this to happen so that the plot can continue."

Of course, Bigfoot revives. George Henderson knows not where the sasquatch's pulse be located. Once introduced into the mild, the gentle woodape upends their refrigerator, eats elder daughter's prized "15-year-old birthday corsage" (leading to outraged teen hilarity), buries a old mink stole in the back yard, is astonished that deer heads mounted on walls don't have the rest of the deer behind, buries that too, and generally destroys the house and everything around it while nine-year-old not-at-all-a-budding-serial-killer four-eyed Ernie howls profanity in

astonishment to the delight of '80s kids everywhere presumably.

Amid the destruction, "Harry", as George dubs him after not deciding to murder the beast in his own home ("George, would you like to shoot him now or wait until you get home?" "Shoot him now! Shoot him now!"), wreaks more havoc, puts Harry-head bumps in the roofs of all their cars, escapes, is reunited with the Family H., but mostly, thanks to an amazing animatronic mask built by Rick Baker and performed beneath by Kevin Peter Hall (who was also *The Predator*), Harry stares at the new world in astonishment and wonder and bewilderment and frustration. This is so the audience can do so too, yet still be amused by the creature's innocent foibles, and can laugh uproariously as Harry launches himself into the air at the command "Sit."

But in the end, the audience is meant, as the Hendersons do, to rethink about our treatment of the environment, of our gun laws and subsequent fetishism of such, of whether or not something is sentient, of whether or not we should mock people who have different beliefs than ours. It packs a lot of these concepts into the package of relatively harmless family entertainment. And it's sometimes very strange to revisit '80s movies who are often such contradictory beasts—sincere in content but cynical in approach, including messages to backmask the true Capitalist motivation for the movie's creation. The '80s movie moguls balanced this dichotomy so well at the time, but the seams are more visible now.

As far as the Cryptid ideologies go, *Harry and the Hendersons* gives

Portrait of an '80s nuclear family: L-R Melinda Dillon, Kevin Peter Hall as "Harry", Margaret Langrick, Joshua Rudoy, and John Lithgow. Photo copyright Amblin Entertainment.

us two characters who believe—Don Ameche's once-esteemed professor was laughed out of academia and opened a Bigfoot souvenir stand, as you do; and David Suchet, a great hunter who has dedicated his life to the ultimate game of hide-and-seek, so desperate to finally prove Bigfoot's existence that he'll kill it on sight!—and they're painted in broad contrasting strokes, their characters given some small subtleties thanks to the actors. Once Harry is sighted around the neighborhood in Act II, all the laughing and rational types flood the Henderson gun store for protection from the wild and vicious beast. So: "It doesn't exist but now it does and obviously it wants to kill us." The normal attitude of a *Simpsons* mob. But the movie's stance is firmly in the "They're Real" stage, with a delightful parting shot showing how Sasquatch(es?) are able to blend so thoroughly with their environment, because they are part of the environment. They respect the world

while we crash and destroy everything in our path—exactly like Harry does when introduced to our "civilization". Which, again, another mixed message: "Respect nature by leaving it the hell alone." Which isn't one I can disagree with.

Ultimately I can understand both ends of the crypto argument. One the one hand, *Harry* and its subsequent three-season TV series run (which I was completely unaware of existing), made Bigfoot popular again. After *Harry*, Bigfoot and Bigfoot-related products were big(foot) business again. So from an awareness-standpoint, *Harry* was a good thing. From another point of view, as my colleague Bill Adcock pointed out earlier, for at least a generation "Harry" was the definitive starting point for sasquatch, both in appearance and temperament, possibly removing some of the wonder and mystery from the creature, having bestowed upon it a faux-Disney status now. For some, *Harry and the Hendersons* somehow *cheapened* Bigfoot.

Still, thirty years later and a nice DVD release later, *Harry and the Hendersons* is a quintessential *E.T.*-clone from the same company who brought you *E.T.* It's never boring, it doesn't ask too much of you or of itself, it hits all the right emotional beats and uses the score appropriately so you don't mistake these beats for anything else; ignore the product placement (it's just what you do), and enjoy the slow enlightenment of a family of upstanding white suburbanites coming to terms with the idea that they may not be the center of the universe they thought they were. (MW)

The Loch Ness Horror (1982)

The Loch Ness Horror is a tepid old school monster movie with the legendary Scottish beastie Nessie rising up from the depths of the famed Loch to take a bite out of anyone she sees as a threat to her eggs. Filmed on location... on Lake Tahoe, California, USA by near-legendary schlockmeister Larry Buchanan (*The Naked Witch*, *Mars Needs Women* and *Mistress of the Apes*).

It all starts out with a prelude that would like us to believe that that a German bomber plane crashed into Loch Ness right by Nessie herself (via some stock footage from *Where Eagles Dare* and a whole lot of wishful thinking on the part of the Larry). It then skips on more modern and sunny times with some poachers finding not only the wrecked bomber (which won't be of much importance until the third act) but also one of Nessie's eggs.

If you find the many Bigfoot films reviewed elsewhere in this fine publication a bit too true to life and realistic this may be the film for you. From the "Scottish" accents of its cast to the Loch Ness monster prop (that would be seen again in *Amazon Woman On The Moon*) not a single thing leads you to believe that any part of the film is really taking place on the famous loch or that the famous monster is real. I must admit that while the *The Loch Ness Horror* doesn't really seem like it's happening in Scotland the film does have some gorgeous location work and looks beautiful. Unfortunately the lovely Tahoe vistas make it seem more like someone's vacation footage or a promotion for a tourist destination than a horror film. The film is also bloated with subplots and filler making it seem much longer than it is, and did the film really need a third act WWII scandal thrown into the mix with characters that had really nothing to do with the rest of the film?

Despite these flaws, like many of Larry Buchanan films, this is oddly watchable if a bit dull. And it may be the only film where a soldier is killed by a Nessie head butt. It's a shame that Larry didn't make a Bigfoot film to pair with this at the drive in. (MH)

The Mothman Prophesies (2002).

Washington Post journalist John Klein (Richard Gere) is house hunting with his wife when their car strikes something in the road. Wife Mary (Debra Messing) hits her head and a subsequent CAT scan reveals a tumor. While in the last throes of her life, she compulsively draws a dark, shadowy winged creature, presumably the thing she saw at the time of the accident. Two years later, while driving to Virginia, John loses two hours of time and winds up in Point Pleasant, WV, four hundred miles from his destination. His car breaks down without explanation and seeking help from a local farm house, the man inside, Gordon (Will Patton) holds him at gunpoint until the Officer Connie (Laura Linney) arrives. According to the homeowner, John has been at the house pounding on the door for three nights in a row. Of course, John has never stepped foot in Point Pleasant before.

It seems as though the entire town of Point Pleasant has been plagued recently with "weirdness". Odd phone calls with whispering voices or strange machinery noises ring at all hours of the day and night. A bright light leaves a young man with retinal damage. Connie herself had a dream where she's drowning, but a voice tells her, "Wake up, Number 37." Meanwhile, Gordon is visited by the man he thought was John, but is in fact a being named "Indrid Cold" (director Mark Pellington in the most egregious cameo since Cecil B. DeMille declared that only he sounded enough like God for *The Ten Commandments*), who does not exist in our reality, and what he looks like "depends on who is looking."

Cold gives a vague warning that many will die "over the river Ohio", leading John to believe a chemical plant is about to explode. The true horror is that he's off by several miles, and that the Silver Bridge is due to collapse—without warning and without explanation.

Except that in 1971, the reason given for the Silver Bridge's collapse was "stress corrosion cracking in an eyebar in a suspension chain," giving lie to the film's final title card that "the collapse was never explained." Which is just the first of many lies and faulty connections making up the tenuous thread that is the plot of *The Mothman Prophesies*. Based on John Keel's hysteria-based book and updated for modern times, the movie asks that the viewer suspend all disbelief to buy into the central conceit that an alien periodically warns us about pending disasters, but not in a way that anyone can do anything about it. Or even understand the warning until it's too late. Alan Bates, as the obligatory discredited expert, tells John, "Do you ever explain yourself to a cockroach?" Which is a pretty off-handed way of dismissing an alien that might just be getting off on trolling West Virginia.

The stars of this film are not Gere or Linney, but Fred Murphy's cinematography and Brian Berdan's erratic editing, keeping the moody film off balance and doing its best to propel the sluggish pacing forward. Lots of deep, meaningful stares from Gere. Lots of concerned looks from Linney. There are numerous creepy moments to be sure—John is constantly getting phone calls from people who are not home. John himself appears to people when he has not left his room. Phone calls come from the future. From the dead. One plot point echoes the *Monkey's Paw*, as Indred Cold leaves him a note telling him to be back in Georgetown to receive a call from his late wife, and John is frozen in horror when the phone actually does begin to ring. All of this leads up to an exciting and devastating bridge collapse at the end, leaving thirty-six people dead. Leaving no question as to who "Number 37" was meant to be.

The biggest problem with *The Mothman Prophesies* is it takes no stance on the creature's veracity and there's no dénouement showing how John or Connie, or the rest of the town, dealt with the Mothman's aftermath. We're told it never visited Point Pleasant again but instead has gone on some world tour, always preceding some terrible accident. It's as if the film itself is embarrassed to admit—or not—that The Mothman is a real entity. Now, I'm a big fan of ambiguity, but don't introduce plot points and then tell me they don't matter. At least *The X-Files* gives you monsters to look at and doubt. *The Mothman Prophesies* gives us glowing eyes and flashes of silver before settling on Richard Gere's sleepy face for two hours. Perhaps a more dynamic actor would have given the narrative a greater sense of urgency, but when your main character does little more than stare and mumble, you're not left with a great deal to latch onto. You start hoping your own phone would ring— even if the voice on the other end belongs to the ludicrously-monikered "Ingrid Cold". (MW)

Savage (2011)

As firefighters try to contain a raging forest fire in the Bear Valley National Park the animals are being forced out of their natural habitats, including a beast that was better left alone. Now the legendary tourist attraction has the town under siege and head ranger Owen Fremont (Tony Becker, Tour of Duty) needs to find a way to stop the creature's rampage before any more lives are lost.

Savage is by far one of the best Bigfoot movies I have seen right up there with *Abominable* and *Dark Was The Night*. It is a bit more serious than most of the other Bigfoot movies and lets say sincere. Lets face it a lot of times Bigfoot comes across as kind of hokey(and those messin with sasquatch slim jim commercials don't help his image at all) But that's not the case in *Savage,* no sir. In *Savage* Bigfoot is a mean freaking killing machine. In fact he racks up a kill count that would make a Predator proud. The CGI that brings him to life are not the greatest but they are fair and the filmmakers keep his appearances hidden well.

The other thing the film has got going on is a good cast. I know you're thinking lots of Bigfoot films have good casts (kind of odd but seems to be true) and you would be right. But in *Savage* the cast once again is sincerely plying their trade like they were trying to build a resume instead of fill their refrigerator or make a mortgage payment. You've got *The Karate Kid*'s Martin Kove as the crazy hunter with a score to settle with Bigfoot who instead of cheesying it up gives a fairly rounded portrayal of a man having a life long blood feud with the missing link. Tony Becker also is in good form as a former big-city policeman trying to put the violence of the city behind him and start a new life with his pregnant wife (Lisa Wilcox). These two are backed up by a host of other good performers including Anna Enger, Shane Callahan, Charles Landress and Ron Prather

The film is topped off with a faced paced third act and a taut, trapped-in-the-attic climax capped off by a very heart breaking bit of self sacrifice. (MH)

Skulduggery (1970). Not to be confused with the "role-playing terror film" of 1983 (dealing with the dangers of D&D and it's penchant for summoning demons), *Skulduggery* has one of the strangest pedigrees of any junk film: directed by Gordon Douglas (whose career dates back to the Hal Roach era and might be best known for directing *In Like Flint*, as well as nearly a hundred more titles), produced by Saul David (producer of *In Like Flint* and *Fantastic Voyage*), and stars Burt Reynolds, Susan Clark, Edward Fox, and *Star Trek*'s own Harry Mudd, Roger C. Carmel. The screenplay is based on the French novel *Les Animaux dénaturés* (1952) (also known in English as *You Shall Know Them,* and *The Murder of the Missing Link*) by Jean Bruller (writing under the pseudonym "Vercors"). Keep in mind, too, that David and Douglas only got involved after

the original director—Otto fucking Preminger—ultimately bowed out. Both the novel and the movie involve the discovery of a lost race of "missing links", named "Tropi", in Papau, New Guinea. While exploring the nature of the creatures, as well as exploring what makes a primate "human", both the book and the movie descend into some decidedly strange territory to make their points.

Reynolds plays Douglas Temple, a borderline-misogynistic bush pilot who, while not pressuring Clark's respected scientist into sleeping with him, becomes a friend of sorts to the Tropi. Carmel (replacing Karl Malden, judged "too thin" by Douglas) becomes a *true* friend by impregnating one of the Tropi (Pat Suzuki from *The Flower Drum Song* as "Topazia"). Ultimately, Tropazia miscarries, but this leads to an almost literal "Monkey Trial" when Temple confesses to murdering the baby. His motivation for this is to pressure local governments into settling the matter once and for all if the Tropi are, in fact, sentient enough to be considered human, albeit primitive. The resulting trial is an astonishing circus, involving a white colonialist (Wilfred Hyde-White) not only proclaiming the Tropi inferior to man, but also admitting—when confronted by a black revolutionary—that African Americans are substandard as well. And, oh the chaos this leads to!

What makes *Skulduggery* so fascinating, beyond its time-capsule curiosity (particularly as an example of Reynolds' early career as he was still trying to establish his personality brand), is how sincere it tries to be while bungling so much of what it's trying to accomplish. Gordon Douglas is a craftsman director, never showy or very stylish, but he always got the job done. Which is true here, but the script leaps from comic misogyny to comedic monkey antics to stark drama and a little touch of horror (Temple is outraged to discover the Tropi are cannibals—particularly after he accidentally eats a bit of one), culminating in a trial that is meant to be earnest, but can't possibly take a stance one way or another and thus ends with a dismissal (and Tropazia's horrific death). Then the credits roll!

In later years, Burt Reynolds had good things to say about the script and his co-stars, lesser-good things to say about Douglas' direction. And there are good things to be found in here, though in the end it's more a curiosity than anything else. It's never had an "official" DVD release and the prints that can be found are in rough shape. Still, it is worth a look, if only for the jaw dropping trial the tops off the clumsy madness that preceded. (MW)

Snowbeast (1977)

A Colorado ski resort celebrating its 50th winter carnival is besieged by a savage man-eating Yeti/Sasquatch that has made the ski slopes its hunting grounds.

This is a derivative 1977 NBC movie of the week that tried to capitalize on the then current nature-run-amok fad. A Sasquatch that threatens to cut short the big snow festival that keeps the town alive comes so close to Jaws it starts to get funny. It's even more amusing when you do some research and learn that the teleplay was written by Joseph Stefano (who wrote the script *for*

Psycho).reportedly based on a book by Roger Patterson (the same Roger Patterson who in 1967 shot the first "real" footage of bigfoot on film) but it seems much more likely that Joseph read a book by Peter Benchley or perhaps saw some Steven Spielberg film as his primary inspiration. Fairly exciting stuff for a movie of the week and I must point out when the big white Yeti makes his first onscreen appearance bursting through a window it looks almost as real as the one in *Shriek Of The Mutilated.*

What set this apart from at least many of the bigfoot films that would come afterword is it top notch production values and big name star cast. There is a ton of big name talent including Bo Svenson, Yvette Mimieux, Clint Walker, Sylvia Sidney, and Robert Logan. Bo is particularly good as Gar Seberg, an ex olympic gold medalist. He is in great shape in this film and with his tall frame it's easy to believe he was once a championship skier. Clint Walker is also great playing the local sheriff it's pretty much a part that fits him like a glove. Yvette Mimieux however does not fair as well Gar's wife and is trapped in cliche love triangle (with

Here, have a snowbeast. Photo copyright Douglas Cramer Productions. All Rights Reserved.

Robert Logan as the third leg).

Sadly our Snowbeast doesn't really get that much screen time or rack up that many kills either, but as this was a made for tv effort you can't really expect much more than what we got. But hey, look at all them folks skiing, that's cool, right? And those beautiful snow capped mountain vistas that has got to be worth something right? (MH)

Suburban Sasquatch (2004)

When a giant blood-thirsty anthropoid with supernatural powers is driven from its natural habitat by a new land development in *Woodstown Pennsylvania,* a sprawling suburban park area, the beast goes plum crazy, it's up to a couple of rangers (Dave Bonavita and Juan Fernandez), a reporter (Bill Ushler) and a mystical Native-American Warrior(Sue Lynn Sanchez) to try and stop it.

This shot on video micro budget film from actor and director Dave Wascavage (Fungicide) is about a magic Bigfoot (Yeah, magic--this bitch can disappear and reappear at will and may have the power to cloud men's minds) on a backyard killing spree (literally). While I have had some difficulty trying to decide what the high points of Sasquatch-ploitation are, it is pretty easy for me to point out *Suburban Sasquatch* as being one of the low points. This film is just a hot freaking mess, an all you can eat blooper-filled buffet of bad acting, poor editing and horrible practical and digital effects. Where does one even begin....Let's start with the film's title monster--brought to life with a threadbare ape costume that Ed Wood would have passed up-- caves made from tarps, off sized giant

foot props, digital fountains of blood that just disappear, and lost limbs that come and go. Which all adds up to, depending on your mood bad movie gold (next season of MST3K, perhaps?) or a disaster.

I will say this for *Suburban Sasquatch* it does entertain (perhaps not always in a way its filmmakers hoped perhaps but entertaining none the less) and the cast took it all very seriously no matter how ridicules the on screen antics become everyone plays it straight without a single wink at the camera. Also the film is not boring, it might not break any new ground and the script is kind of rough but it moves pretty quick. (MH)

Throwback (2014)

Reviewed by Mike Haushalter

A pair of double crossing treasure hunters (Shawn Brack and Anthony Ring), a beautiful park ranger (Melanie Serafin) and an unhinged ex-cop (Vernon Wells, *The Road Warrior)* tangle with a Yowie, the Australian Bigfoot, deep in the jungles of Queensland in *Throwback,* writer/ director Travis Bain's tribute to Ray Harryhausen.

Throwback opens with a short prelude set in 1825 establishing both of the legends that the film is focused on (which thanks to the video stock used to the film looks very much like a reenactment from Robert Stack's *Unsolved Mysteries*). From there *Throwback* skips ahead to modern days and thanks to the magic of editing the film jumps head long into the hunt for the lost treasure of 'Thunderclap' Newman, gold fever, and a race to escape one very angry man beast.

This is a small budget, Tarantino-

74

esque, fast paced action/horror tale with an offbeat script, a soundtrack courtesy of Richard Band, and fantastic use of outdoor locations. It's not a perfect film and some late in the game casting changes probably didn't help but as I may have mentioned before the bar is really not that high when it comes to the "Bigfoot" genre (or "Sasquatch-ploitation" as the kids may be now calling it) and with that in mind this is a pretty top tier as far as bigfoot films go. It's also chock full of homages and in jokes including a bottle of wine from Boggy Creek and a very nice nod to King Kong.

Yeti: Giant of the 20th Century (1977). Stupid, yet cunning. I can think of no other way to describe the film first unleashed on the world as *Yeti: Il Gigante del 20. Secolo*; the world's yeti craze had died down almost twenty years before, making this film almost seem like a prehistoric throwback itself. But what we're looking at here is less a Yeti movie and more a testament to just how far the Italians would go to rip off a hit. Not content with churning out endless *Jaws* cash-ins and unofficial *Zombie* sequels, what we have here is a rip-off of Dino De Laurentiis' ill-conceived *King Kong*. Yes, you didn't even have to have an actual hit to be ripped off by the Italians.

When multimillionaire Canadian businessman Hunnicutt's nephew finds a 20-foot caveman frozen in a glacier, he turns to his old friend, Professor Waterman, for a professional opinion on thawing the thing out. Once Waterman gets a look at it, he realizes that the caveman is so well-preserved that, if thawed, they might be able to revive him! Naturally, this goes about as well as can be expected, and made a whole lot worse once Hunnicutt's goon-of-all-trades orders his men to fire on the Yeti. The giant turns violent, with his rampage only cut short when he catches sight of the fur-trimmed jackets worn by Hunnicutt's niece Jane and nephew Herbie. Mistaking them for children, the Yeti goes into nurture mode and is recaptured. But between Hunnicutt's greedy plans to make a spokesmonster of the Yeti, and Jane and Waterman's growing conviction that the Yeti must be freed, it's only a matter of time until something goes awry.

Yeti: Giant of the 20th Century is something of a mess. I don't think anyone will argue producing a rip-off of a Kong-sized flop was a good idea in the first place; nevertheless, it happened, and I kind of think we got the best possible outcome. A twenty foot caveman with a bouffant 'do and strong parental instincts is a far cry from the savage man-ape promised by the poster art, or even anything that I would call a yeti. The matte-work is terrible, with the yeti appearing in turn transparent and outlined by a white border, and the less said about the quality of the English-language dub, the better. But you know something? The film tries, goddamn it, and there's a lot of heart to be found here. It's like we're looking at the scrappy underdog of Italian rip-offs, and that counts for something in my book.

I'd Buy That for a Dollar!

Mike Haushalter

One of my favorite activities is to look through bargain bins and the racks of second-hand sellers to find movie deals. Whether it's a forgotten A-list title, blink and you missed it indie release, or last year's hot direct to home video title, as long as it costs 2 to 5 bucks it's bound to come home with me.But if it's less than that? Well, I'm willing to take a gamble on almost anything that's priced at a dollar and offers even a tiny bit of intrigue or interest. After all, I can't even rent most of these things for that price, and if they don't work out, I can sell them again. But when they do work out, it's magical. Here's a roundup of my latest finds, good and bad!

The search for new films for this outing was made more difficult by the fact that my local Exchange stores were so stocked up on dollar movies that it was hard to find things that well were more than just mundane. Tons of the films on the dollar shelf would have cost three to five dollars back when I wrote the last article just a few months ago and anything worth writing about needs to been something someone would be unlikely to buy at all or a surprise to find for a buck.

Scratch: The New Sound of Terror (2004) Aka: Ratten 2: Sie kommen wieder!

The box says: "Get ready for a terrifying tale when a deadly rat plague begins sweeping the nation! After a woman is found bitten to death, Frank and Katrin, who helped defeat the pack of rats in the first rat plague, know something is wrong. And

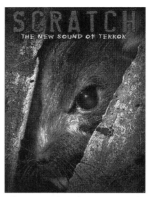

when the rats begin to attack other residents, it is up to them to find the deranged scientist responsible for the genetically mutated rodents.... Before it's too late."

Why I risked a dollar: Killer rodents? I love me a good killer rat movie (if only I could find some). What more do you need? How about the promise of blood and boobs in the parental warning box?

Thoughts: Not the greatest film I have ever seen but it was fun and interesting, and it was more about people stepping up to be heroes than a movie about a bunch of unlikeable folks being set up as rat bait.

Plus: Decent characters, lots and lots of creepy rats, bit of bare flesh

Minus: Dubbing could put some people off, Could have used a lot more blood. And it has that over filtered drab brown kind of look for far too many scenes.

Shelf/Bin: Up in the air on this one, I liked it enough to seek out the film that came before it. If the first one is as good or better than this I think I might keep, but if the first doesn't live

76

up to its sequel then there's a good chance I will bin them both.

Follow-up: So I picked up the first film *Revenge of the Rats* from Amazon for a bit more than a dollar and gave it a view. It was not quite as fun as its sequel but it was another decent killer rat outing.

Vendetta for The Saint (1969)

The box says: Roger Moore stars as Simon Templar in Vendetta for the Saint (1969). Simon Templar is stylish, sophisticated and seemingly wealthy, yet his past is shrouded in mystery.

Based upon the book by Leslie Charteris, Vendetta for The Saint involves Templar in a deadly case of mistaken identity. While in Italy, Templar encounters Alessandro Destamio (well known British character actor Ian Hendry), who claims he's from an aristocratic Italian family, yet a bank manager believes him to be Dino Cardelli, a former bank clerk. When the bank manager is found murdered, The Saint is determined to discover Destamio's true identity.

Templar befriends Destamio's terrified girlfriend, Lily (Aimi Macdonald) and soon lands in jail on false charges. A local investigator, Marco Ponti (George Pastell), orders his release and warns him he's come up against the Sicilian mafia. It's a critical time for the crime family- Don Pasquale (Finlay Currie) is dying and Destamio wants the job. As Templar risks his life to prove that Destamio is really Cardeli, he survives multiple assassination attempts, plants a seed of doubt about Destamio in Don Pasquale's mind and enlists beautiful women to help solve the case.

Directed by Jim O'Connolly. Written by Harry W. Junkin and John Kruse. Produced by Robert S. Baker.

Why I risked a dollar: I was depression shopping just a few hours after learning of the passing of Sir Roger Moore, a man who had long been one of my heroes, and I found this. Just seemed like I was meant to see it.

Thoughts: Wow. This was really good. I had not really seen much of Roger Moore's work on The Saint other than a few chance encounters on TV but this was a really decent movie built from TV episodes.

Plus: A young, top-of-his-game Roger Moore. Great supporting cast. Good script. A nice punch up and a surprisingly violent ending. Also the disc had and audio commentary with Roger Moore.

Minus: Some very noticeable sets. If you're not a Roger Moore fan this might not be for you.

Shelf/Bin: Shelf, in fact strongly considering just buying the box set of The Saint.

Delivery (2006)

The box says: "We deliver in 30 minutes or your killing is free. Everybody orders pizza

delivery. But when your pizza arrives, who is that you're opening your door to? Is it a nice kid looking to make a few bucks.... or is it Monty?"

Montgomery Goth (Matt Nelson) is a gentle loner with a traumatic past, trying to put the pieces of his life back together while working as a delivery boy for a local pizza place. He has no friends, no life, and no prospects for the future until one day he meets the girl of his dreams, Bibi (Tara Cardinal), and life seems to finally change for the better. But a series of events will test Montgomery's sanity and awaken the demons inside of him, unleashing a murderous rampage that will keep everyone from ordering delivery for a very long, long time...

Why I risked a dollar: Cover art and tagline pretty much sold me on this one.

Thoughts: This is an award winning debbie downer micro-budget horror effort about a disturbed loner pushed to the edge by the customers he delivers pizza to. It's a very cruel mix of horror and humor that just does not gel for me. This was a tough one to sit through; not a bad film, but it is just so relentlessly cruel to its marginal hero Montgomery Goth (Matthew Nelson) that I didn't enjoy it. It's easy to see where the film was heading pretty

early on and that we were not taking the quick and comfortable route to the climax. but it did have one of the best put downs I have heard in years: "You couldn't get laid in a women's prison with a fistful of pardons"

Plus: Lots and lots of nudity. Over–the-top kills and not only does this guy deliver he kills in bulk.

Minus: Lots of unlikeable characters. Some very cheesy special effects.

Shelf/Bin: This may be the kind of horror that the kids are eating up these days but it is straight to the bin for me. It is far too mean-spirited for my tastes.

Dark Descent (2002)
Aka: Descent Into Darkness

The box says: "Will anyone be able to reach the surface... Alive? Something is killing undersea miners in the Mariana Sea Basin. Officer William Murdock (Dean Cain, *Lois and Clark*) of the Deep Submersible Division is enlisted to investigate. Things are not what he expected at 35,000 feet below; 24-hour darkness, decompression sickness and a ticking clock of acute claustrophobia intensify the miners' growing rage. It's a race against time as the body count rises.

Can Murdock save the lives of the miners, and ultimately himself?"

Why I risked a dollar: I thought it was a underwater monster-on-the-loose *Alien* clone. I am a big fan of monsters in small places killing-off trapped stupid folk one by one.

Thoughts: Turns out I was completely wrong about this being an *Alien* clone. It is in fact an underwater remake of *Outland*, (which was a remake of High Noon) with Dean Cain as the Marshal with no one to turn to. All-in-all this is not such a bad film and completely worth a dollar.

Plus: Dean Cain is the best part of this film, He is no Sean Connery, of course, but he really shines. There also a few good fire fights and some clever kills.

Minus: No monsters, and since I bought this thinking it was a monster movie and not an underwater western is a pretty big minus. Some very stupid decisions made by characters who seem like they should know better.

Shelf/Bin: This is going right in the bin. I already have a copy of *Outland* and don't need another. Honestly if it had been a monster on the loose flick it might have been a keeper.

A Minute To Pray, A Second To Die. (1968)

The box says: "Old habits die fast in this "brutal, violent (and) intensely realistic' (Boxoffice) western about a desperate gunslinger who's hunted by the law... and haunted by the past! Staring Alex Cord, Arthur Kennedy and Nicoletta Machiavelli. *A Minute To Pray, A Second To Die* is heavily armed with "great atmosphere" (Leonard Maltin) and "shoot- 'em-up action" (Variety) "from breathtaking

beginning... to "explosive climax" (Boxoffice)!"

When Clay McCord (Cord), the fastest draw in the west, gets the shakes in his shooting arm he decides to hang up his guns for good. But riding the straight and narrow may be more dangerous than he ever imagined--especially when his only hope for survival lies in the hands of a shady sheriff who's offer of amnesty hides something far more deadly!

Why I risked a dollar: To be honest the film was on my Amazon wish list and had been on my radar so long I do not remember any more why I wanted to see it in the first place.

Thoughts: After watching this I am still not sure why I wanted to see it. The film is average spaghetti western hokum with a strong cast but listless plotting and characters.

Plus: Decent cast, plenty of wild west gunplay, and Alex Cord is good.

Minus: Weak murky plot, thin characters, Alex Cord has almost no one to work against till the last reel, and seemingly important characters die off screen.

Shelf/Bin: This was definitely a "one watch and done." In fact it's already in the bin bag for the next trade in trip.

ABOUT OUR CONTRIBUTORS:

Bill Adcock was raised on a steady diet of old monster movies and just look what it did to him. Self-described as reclusive and long-suffering, he requires little provocation to go off at length about gorilla suits, gill-men, and the filmography of Uschi Digard. When not watching utter trash, he can be found talking to his cat like it's people.

Dr. Rhonda Baughman is a writer and educator, currently resides in Colorado Springs, CO. She has written for *Sirens of Cinema, Film Threat, Grindhouse Purgatory,* and is the author of the novella, *My Transvestite: A Novella of Love and Death, Pornography and Revolution.*

Mike Haushalter is a lifetime fan and student of film. A genre film reviewer for *Drive-In Asylum, Grindhouse Purgatory,* and *Weng's Chop.* He is the publisher, writer, and publicity for *Secret Scroll Digest.*

Bill Hahner is a Corgi-enthusiast and a snappy dresser from the turn-of-the-century. He is a renowned illustrator ruthlessly badgered into contributing to this issue.

Ryan Hose is a graphic designer and illustrator in the Pittsburgh area, specializing in vector graphics, pencil renderings, and quirky layouts. He will talk endlessly about music. Check out his portfolio at behance.net/ryandennis923f

Philip R. Rogers, pusher of pixels, Rogers lives in the frightening wilds of western North Carolina. His wife Janet constantly inspires and encourages him. They share their home with a passel of cats and one skeleton affectionately called "Mr. Bones". Check out more of his work at http://www.philiprrogers.com.

Douglas Waltz resides in the wilds of Kalamazoo Michigan and when he's not working on his own 'zine, *Divine Exploitation,* he contributes to *Grindhouse Purgatory, Monster!, Weng's Chop,* In the land of fiction his recent releases are *Thou Shalt Not Live!, Sasquatch Vs. The Blind Dead* and *Killer F**king Squirrels.*

William J. Wright is a Rondo Hatton Classic Horror Award nominated journalist and critic specializing in horror and cult entertainment. His work has appeared in *Phantom of the Movies' Videoscope, Penny Blood, Sirens of Cinema, Fangoria.com, Stiff, Dread Central* and *Film Threat,* among others. In addition to his print work, he produces and co-hosts the MORTIS horror podcast. (wm.j.wright@gmail.com, mortiscontact@gmail.com)

NEXT ISSUE: THE CRAZIEST MOVIES IN CINEMA HISTORY!

22296709R00047

Printed in Poland
by Amazon Fulfillment
Poland Sp. z o.o., Wrocław